Missing
Children

SUNY Series,
The Psychology of Women
Michele A. Paludi, Editor

Missing Children

A Psychological Approach to Understanding
the Causes and Consequences of Stranger and
Non-Stranger Abduction of Children

James N. Tedisco
and
Michele A. Paludi

STATE UNIVERSITY OF NEW YORK PRESS

Cover art generously provided courtesy of Dynamic Graphics Inc., Peoria, IL.
Copyright, 1988, all rights reserved.

Production by Ruth Fisher
Marketing by Theresa Abad Swierzowski

Published by
State University of New York Press, Albany

© 1996 State University of New York

For information, address the State University of New York Press,
State University Plaza, Albany, NY 12246

Library of Congress Cataloging-in-Publication Data

Tedisco, James N.
    Missing children : a psychological approach to understanding the
causes and consequences of stranger and non-stranger abduction of
children / James N. Tedisco and Michele A. Paludi.
        p.   cm. — (SUNY series, the psychology of women)
    Includes bibliographical references and index.
    ISBN 0-7914-2879-6 (hardcover : acid-free). — ISBN 0-7914-2880-X
(pbk. : acid-free)
    1. Abduction—United States. 2. Abduction—United States—
Psychological aspects. 3. Abduction—United States—Prevention.
I. Paludi, Michele Antionette. II. Title. III. Series: SUNY series
in the psychology of women.
HV6574.U6T43   1996
    613.6—dc20   95-18494
                                                                 CIP

10 9 8 7 6 5 4 3 2 1

For children and adolescents and their families:
Our hope and our prayers

Contents

Foreword

Nothing electrifies and frightens everyone in a community like the kidnapping of a child from our midst. From a street just like yours. Perhaps a child just like yours.

When a child is abducted an entire community suffers. Friends, neighbors, even casual acquaintances rally round the afflicted family. Community members are both horrified and frightened for the safety of their own children.

So great is America's concern for children that cases of abduction make the national news. Yet in spite of the attention following an abduction, no real profile of the abductor or abductee has been written. Tedisco and Paludi's *Missing Children* makes an important contribution to the subject.

When I first came to the capital region of New York State, the disappearance of Sara Anne Wood spotlighted the horror of this subject. Images of her father, community members, police officers, and other searchers combing endless cold acres of Adirondack forests in the futile search for her body were shown on the nightly news.

When a child in Pittsfield, Massachusetts, escaped a would-be abductor by using techniques learned in an anti-abduction class at school, I began soliciting listeners to my radio show on WGY in Albany, New York, to write and call the Governor and legislators in support of James Tedisco's proposed abduction avoidance curriculum. I am proud to have been of some assistance to him in obtaining passage of that legislation.

This book is a natural extension of Jim's commitment to the cause of understanding abduction of children. Michele

Paludi's collaboration with him as his legislative advisor on women's issues, plus her background as a psychologist, college teacher, and author, contributes to making *Missing Children* an authoritative work. It should be required reading for parents, police officers, school administrators, faculty and students, as well as state and national legislators.

Myrna Lamb
Albany, New York

Preface

There's more than anger, more than sadness, more than terror. There's hope.—Edith Horning, cited in Bass & Davis, 1988.

Recently, I was reminded of these words of Edith Horning when I was asked by an interviewer to share an experience with the listening audience that I considered to be a miracle.

The miracle in my life thus far centered around my appointment in 1984 as the chair of the New York State Assembly Republican Task Force on Missing Children. The task force held statewide public hearings to gether information from individuals who testified about their experiences with missing children and their families, peers, and teachers. Throughout each of the hearings in New York State, individuals highlighted the need for support in locating missing children—displaying pictures/descriptions of missing children in post offices—and developing significant legislation to address the issue.

This request on the part of individuals providing us with testimony was utmost on my mind as I drove to and from my office each day. One morning, as I was en route to the assembly I got on the thruway in Schenectady, got my ticket and proceeded to Albany. A few hundred feet away from the toll both I pulled my car over and reviewed the ticket I has just been given. Why not put pictures of missing children on the back of toll tickets in New York State? The prospect of this idea becoming a reality was exciting for me. When I got to my office I discussed the idea with my colleagues, including representatives for Governor Mario Cuomo, and within a few weeks the first picture of a missing child, a young girl, was placed on the back of toll tickets in New York State. New York thus became the first state in the nation to use its transportation system as a way of locating missing children.

Edith Horning's words were beginning to take on more meaning for me with the governor and the entire legislature supporting my suggestion.

> There's more than anger, more than sadness, more than terror.
>
> There's hope.

This isn't the end of my "miracle" story, however. The first girl whose picture we placed on the toll tickets in New York State was found three weeks after we initiated this procedure. Her recovery is truly a miracle and gave me great hope in our efforts to deal with child abductions and missing children. I have carried this first toll ticket around with me in my appointment book since 1984 as a symbol of hope and the importance of individuals working together, regardless of political affiliations, to help with the problem of missing children.

This still isn't the end of my miracle story. A few years ago, while campaigning door-to-door for my reelection to the assembly, I rang a doorbell on one home and was quickly invited into the house. As I entered the house, I saw a young woman of about sixteen sitting with her father. On the wall behind the young woman hung the picture of the seven-year-old girl on the toll ticket. Yes, this was the girl who had been found with the assistance of New York State's transportation system. As I shook her hand and heard the tremendous amount of appreciation in her family's voices, I took out my copy of the toll ticket from my appointment book and shared the feelings of joy I had experienced when this young woman had been found and brought back to the safety and love of her family. I also told them that if I never accomplish anything else in my tenure as a member of the state legislature, at least I know I had helped bring this woman and her family back together. Meeting this young woman nearly ten years after her abduction gave me an enormous sense of hope.

When I talk with mothers and fathers of missing children to this day, I remember our first success story and try to remind the family that yes, they should be angry that their child is missing. And yes, they should also be saddened at the loss of seeing, hearing, and talking with their child, watching her or him grow. And, yes, the mothers and fathers should sense the terror their child may be experiencing with an abductor and/or from being apart from their loved ones. But, I also tell mothers and fathers to have hope in their child, in themselves, and in the many hundreds of individuals who are all working together to bring their child back home.

It is because Michele Paludi and I truly believe in this sentiment that we wanted to write this book.

James N. Tedisco
Schenectady, New York

Acknowledgments

We would like to thank the following individuals for their support, encouragement, and advice during the writing of this book:

Thomas Tedisco

Beatrice Tedisco

Howard Becker

Shirley DeMartino

Rosalie Paludi

Lucille Paludi

Lois Patton

Clarence D. Rappleyea

and

The New York State Minority Task Force on Child Abduction and Missing Children

Introduction

Although generalizations are difficult given some problems in identifying children as "missing" or "abducted," the best estimate is that child abductions is the most widespread of all forms of child victimization studied.

In 1992 a total of 27,553 cases of missing children were reported in New York State through the Missing Children Register. The majority of missing children cases involved suspected runaways. Abduction cases accounted for 1 percent of the total report; those committed by family members comprised the most frequent form of abduction (as opposed to abduction by strangers). In addition, 88 percent of the children reported missing were thirteen or older, 60 percent were girls, and 58 percent were white. The single largest group of cases involved white girls between the ages of thirteen and fifteen.

Researchers have clearly established that child abductions are not usually sexually motivated, but are a violent way to achieve a sense of power. Case studies support a similar psychological mechanism among child abductors. Abductors use the advantage of their physical strength over their victims, or wield a gun or a knife. Abductors also use age, social position, economic power, authority, and/or manipulative lures as their weapons. They rely on their victims' fear, vulnerability, and obedience to adults' authority. Child abductors are characteristically habitual offenders and carry out their assaults in a highly stereotypical modus operandi.

The abduction of a child has a radiating impact and can thus affect the life experiences of all those in the child's community, transforming parents, siblings, friends, and teachers into victims also. It is inevitable that once victimized in this way, at minimum, one can never again feel quite as invulnerable.

Child abduction is a serious socioeconomic problem. To date there is no text that addresses the incidence, psychological dimensions, and explanatory models of child abductions. This book fills a need in the literature on child abductions and missing children by focusing on variables that can assist communities in confronting and preventing child abductions. These variables include teacher training, public education and awareness, and psychotherapeutic techniques for families and friends of abducted children, as well as the children themselves.

Part one begins with an exploration of the myths individuals hold about missing children and child abductions. Part two consists of a discussion of the three types of missing children: runaways, stranger abductions, and noncustodial abductions. For each of these types of missing children we integrate the legal and psychological approaches to understanding the occurrence of these behaviors. Part three centers around parents and teachers educating children and adolescents about safety with respect the child abductions. An overview of current legislation in New York State as well as other states is also provided. Suggestions for curriculum integration projects are also offered for teachers of elementary and secondary school students.

The best protection individuals can give children lies in the power of understanding and education. It is the hope of the authors that parents, teachers, and other concerned individuals who read this book can successfully impart this information to the children in their lives.

REFERENCE

Bass, E., & L. Davis. (1988). *The Courage to Heal: Women Healing from Child Sexual Abuse.* New York: Harper & Row.

Part One

Introduction to the Psychology of Child Abductions

1

Perceptions and Realities

INTRODUCTION: WE SEE WHAT WE EXPECT TO SEE

James Tedisco's brother, Thomas, is an amateur magician with an interest in illusion. He is a good sleight of hand magician who has mastered basic vanishes. He gives the illusion that an object—for example, a coin—has been passed from the left hand to the right hand when in fact the object is retained by his left hand. When showing this vanish, Tom performs the move and then shows his right hand empty. He thus implies by this gesture that he has vanished the coin. It is a form of misdirection. He makes it look quite natural—as if the coin were actually passed. He actually retains the coin—in his left palm. Tom argues that this illusion is successful because his audience expects him to pass the coin from one hand to the other, based on past experience. Tom reinforces his audience's expectation by his natural moves back and forth with the coin. His move of palming the coin is not detectable to his audience. He has often reminded me of the basic tenet of vanishes: that present perception is built on past experience. Another way of stating this is that individuals see what they expect to see.

We are often reminded of Tom's visual illusions when confronted with educating parents, an interested public, teachers, and children about child abductions. Individuals cling to certain beliefs, based on past experiences, about what child is likely to be abducted, who is likely to be a child abductor, and the role that educators can play in confronting and eliminating child abductions. People see the issues surrounding child abductions the way they expect to see them. Individuals base their opinions on illusions—not visual, but cognitive. They may believe that child abductors are "psychotic," refuse to believe that child abductors are repeat offenders, and believe in seductive childhood sexuality.

The similarity of a magician's vanishing coins to missing or vanished children is apt. People typically don't see what is really there; they cling to illusions. In this chapter we will review some major myths and provide examples of their impact on treatment and reactions of victims. Specifically, we will address the following illusions or myths that relate to either abductors/abusers or victims:

> An abductor is a psychotic human being, easily identifiable by children and adults.
> There are no long-term aftereffects of abductions for those who are found.
> It is only young, helpless children who are the prey of abductors.
> Runaway children and adolescents are not targeted for abductions.
> Parental abduction is not a serious matter and is not a form of child abuse.
> Abductions don't happen here to the people I know— they happen somewhere else.

We will highlight how these popular myths are so pervasive that they confuse individuals about child abductions and missing children. The mythology that is created about this topic can help to "explain away" child abductions or to diminish their damage to victims and to victims' families and friends. Thus, these myths must be tested against reality and debunked.

MYTH: AN ABDUCTOR IS A PSYCHOTIC HUMAN BEING, EASILY IDENTIFIABLE BY CHILDREN AND ADULTS

People want to cling to the illusion that abductors are insane, bizarre, or psychotic. Exceptions to these myths are quite difficult for some to accept. Individuals do not want to believe that a "normal" person could abduct teenage children, especially their own sons or daughters. As Kenneth Lanning (1994) recently pointed out, individuals believe child molesters are sinister indivuals who hang around school playgrounds waiting to lure children with candy.

The illusion that there is a "typical" abuser/abductor who can be identified by his blatant mistreatment of children or adolescents is an oversimplification of a complex issue. While it may be difficult for us to confront the reality that abductions are perpetrated by individuals who are familiar to us, who have family lives similar to ours and who appear to be caring and sensitive individuals, it is a reality.

Psychologists Kathryn Quina and Nancy Carlson (1989) have identified the following common features abductors share: (1) apparent normalcy, (2) repeat offenses, (3) use of a modus operandi, (4) motivation by anger and a need for power, and (5) victims of sexual abuse.

Apparent Normalcy

Sexual abuse and control are to a great degree a part of the abduction process.

Beneke (1982), upon his first meeting with convicted sexual offenders, reported: "The first experience I had was blinding: a feeling of identification. . . . They were not different from the men I knew. They could've been my brother, . . . my father, . . . my friends, . . . me" (41). The vast majority of abductors and abusers are individuals who, unlike the individuals Beneke described, never come to the attention of authorities, are even more likely to seem normal.

This feature of apparent normalcy perhaps can help us to understand why individuals—especially children—may go with a stranger or noncustodial parent. Children often believe they can easily identify an abductor—someone who is sinister and offers "goodies." Children are taught to respect adults, especially adults' authority, and to only talk to people who look "nice." Indeed John Walsh, father of Adam Walsh, an abducted boy who was murdered, once stated that he wished he and his wife had spent more time encouraging Adam to respect his safety instead of respecting adults' authority: "If I had taught him to scream, he might be alive now" (quoted in Gelman, 1984, 86). Victims' faith in their own judgment about other people can be shattered, and often survivors report that "they don't know who to trust anymore" (Quina and Carlson, 1989). They question what is normal and who can be trusted long into their adult years. Indeed, the abductor/abuser's apparent normalcy may lead an adolescent or young adult to question his or her own perceptions of the abuse—did it happen this way or did he or she imagine that this nice man or woman was so violent? This may be fueled by contact with an abductor who acts as if nothing has happened.

Children and adolescents quite frequently experience a split reality—other people in their environment tell them continuously how lucky they are to have such a wonderful parent or friend. They themselves may come to reframe the victimization, perhaps blaming themselves, perhaps believing that all children or adolescents have similar experiences.

Repeat Offenses with a Modus Operandi

In 1991, talk show host Oprah Winfrey urged Congress to adopt a national system of background checks of child-care workers to identify child abusers. She stated:

> Nothing angers me more than to hear a story of a child being abused, assaulted, raped, murdered by someone who had a previous conviction for child abuse, plea bargained, was released and came out to molest and murder a four-year-old girl who lived across the hall—quoted in (*Family Violence and Sexual Assault Bulletin,* 1991, 19).

Winfrey was referring to the experiences of Angelica Mena, who was molested, strangled and thrown into Lake Michigan by a convicted, repeat child molester.

Winfrey's concerns are wellfounded. For example, Abel (1986) reported that 400 child molesters he had interviewed admitted to him to more than 67,000 instances of child abductions and child sexual abuses, representing an average of 117 child victims per molester. Other researchers have reported results similar to Abel's (e.g., Freeman-Longo and Wall, 1986;

Rosenfeld, 1985). And, most abductors/abusers have committed hundreds of abuses for fifteen years or more prior to their first arrests. The low likelihood of "being caught" and relatively nonstringent punishment once incarcerated reinforce repeat offending. Quina and Carlson (1989) reported that the average prison sentence for convicted child sex abusers is less than one year; for convicted rapists, less than five years. Christine Courtois (1988) argued that the child is

> manipulated by the unequal power in the relationship, that is by the relationship with the perpetrator on whom she [sic] is dependent. The child is further coerced by the perpetrator's strong desire to keep the activity a secret, which has the purpose of minimizing intervention and allowing repetition. (6)

Part of the explanation for the repeat offenses concerns the abductor/abuser's modus operandi. Child sexual abusers exhibit consistencies in the cycle of frequency of abuse/abductions, the planning of the abduction/abuse, the approach to the victim—the "lure"—and the behaviors during the abduction and subsequent abuse. Burgess and Holmstrom (1974) identified two types of modus operandi that can apply to child abductors/abusers: the "blitz attack" and the "confidence" or "con" assault.

In the blitz attack, a stranger appears suddenly. Children's responses resemble reactions to any other sudden, unexpected, dangerous event in their lives: (1) they are in so much shock that it interferes with any defensive action they might take; (2) the shock of the stranger's behavior precludes seeing or remembering much of the incident, so that they may have considerable difficulty in recognizing and identifying the individual at a later time; and (3) they label the experience as an assault and themselves as survivors. They may direct anger inward as they self-blame for not defending themselves. A blitz attack may or may not include assault with a weapon.

In the confidence or con assault, however, an elaborate scheme is set up by the abductor/abuser. This is a psychological assault rather than physical assault. Lanning (1994) describes this type of abductor as a "pied piper" who attracts children. Indeed child abductors, especially those who are pedophiles (an individual who prefers to have sex with a child; see chapter 3), usually identify with children better than with adults. This characteristic makes most abductors master seducers of children—they know how to listen to children.

The con assault usually has as its first requirement gaining the confidence of the targeted child/adolescent. The target's trust is used to manipulate her or him into physical and psychological vulnerability. The victim begins to notice a change in the behavior of the abductor from a nice person to an aggressor. However, by the time this realization takes place, the abductor has already assessed his or her potential for escape; many of the child's options are thus eliminated. Trust is devastated after such a con assault. The key to continuing the con assault is to have the abuser convince the victim that he or she is a participant in the crime; that he or she shares the responsibility for the abuse or has no other alternatives. Quina and Carlson (1989) illustrate this psychological manipulation with a description from a reporter's interview with a child molester. The reporter used the pretext of "learning the ropes" from an experienced molester:

> The man, who bragged of abusing dozens of young children, advised him not to do it just once, because in time they might tell, to do it several times right away, because then they will start to believe they have participated and that they carry some of the responsibility. (25)

Many abuctors refer to children as projects, objects, or possessions. Lanning (1994) offered the following typical comments from pedophiles: "This kid has low mileage"; "I've been working on this project for six months" (14). Child abductors are usually skilled in identifying vulnerable victims. They can watch a group of children for a brief period of time and then select a potential target. In many cases their target is from a dysfunctional family and may already be the victim of sexual and/or physical abuse.

Power and Anger, Not Sex

Very few abductors are motivated by sexual needs. On the contrary, abusers have noted in interviews that sexual satisfaction is absent in their abuse of children or adolescents. If any sexual satisfaction does occur, it is in conjunction with the humiliation of the victim and is inseparable from psychological needs (Doyle and Paludi, 1995). The abuser's primary motivation is the feeling of power, one that is rooted in dominance and humiliation of others who are less powerful (e.g., a child). One prime ingredient in sexual abuses is the element of aggression that is deeply embedded in the masculine gender role in North American culture (Doyle and Paludi, 1992).

For men who sexually abuse children, adolescents, or adults, aggression is one of the major ways of proving their masculinity, especially among those men who feel some sense of powerlessness in their lives. Diana Russell (1973) addressed this theme with respect to rape when she stated that rape is not the act of a "disturbed" man but rather an act of an "over-conforming" man. Russell's perspective can be extended to other forms of child abductors as well:

> To win, to be superior, to be successful, to conquer—all demonstrate masculinity to those who subscribe to common cultural notions of masculinity, i.e., the masculine mystique. And it would be surprising if these notions of masculinity did not find expression in men's sexual behavior. Indeed, sex may be the arena where these notions of masculinity are most intensely played out, particularly by men who feel powerless in the rest of their lives, and hence, whose masculinity is threatened by this sense of powerlessness. (1)

Abductors/abusers may fuse aggression and sexuality. Research that examines men's sexual arousal as stimulated by graphic scenes of sexual violence suggests that men—even men who have never committed an act of sexual abuse—report a heightened sexual arousal from these scenes and an increase in their abuse fantasies (Malamuth and Check, 1981). Another disquieting research finding is that when nonabusive men were shown depictions of sexual assault, they reported the possibility that they would even consider using force themselves in their sexual relations. Thus, sexuality is related at some level to an expression of aggression, and in turn aggression heightens men's sexual fantasies or actual sexual behaviors (Malamuth and Donnerstein, 1982). This finding does seem to suggest that one possible way to reduce the sexual violence in our culture against children (as well as adult women) would be to eliminate violent pornography.

Abductors are usually skilled at manipulating children. They use seduction techniques, competition, peer pressure, motivation techniques, and threats to get children to comply with their requests to engage in sex, steal, abuse drugs, or participate in prostitution or pornography. Part of the manipulation process involves lowering the inhibitions of children. This may be accomplished by showing sexually explicit material to children.

MYTH: THERE ARE NO LONG-TERM AFTEREFFECTS OF ABDUCTIONS FOR THOSE WHO ARE FOUND

Considerable research on missing children and sexually abused children and adolescents (see Conte and Berliner, 1988; Finkelhor and Browne, 1988) indicates the extent of psychological damage that can be caused by these forms of victimization. Salasin (1981) suggested that unlike physical abuse and neglect of children, where the evidence may be apparent, psychological problems are subtle and may not surface for some years. Psychological mistreatment is rarely addressed by the courts or by child protective services.

Psychologist Lenore Walker (1992) identified three domains that are affected by psychological damage resulting from abductions and sexual abuse: what individuals think (cognitive), how they feel (affect), and what they do (behavior). Young children and adolescents who have been victimized may not be able to verbalize the impact of the abuse on them until much later in their lives. With respect to the cognitive impact, victims of abductions and abuse initially believe that the victimization will stop. When the abductor's behavior escalates, the victim begins to feel powerless. Subsequent to the abductor's continuing behavior, victims feel trapped. A sense of learned helplessness sets in—that no matter what she or he does, the victimization will not cease. Once individuals recognize that they were legitimate victims who were not to blame for their abduction and abuse, anxiety often shifts to anger.

With respect to the affective impact of abductions and abuse, among the emotional reactions reported by victims of abductions were anger, fear, anxiety, irritability, loss of self-esteem, feelings of humiliation and alienation, and a sense of vulnerability. In addition, most victims experience an immediate postvictimization generalized distress response characterized as a state of psychological shock (e.g., repeated reexperiencing of the trauma by intrusive waking images or dreams, depression and emotional numbing). Victims may not resolve the immediate distress but instead develop a chronic symptom picture that may persist for a considerable length of time.

Psychologist Mary Koss (1990) reported that several random community surveys have found that adult women who were victims of child sexual abuse had identifiable degrees of impairment when compared with nonvictims. For example, 17 percent of adult women abused as children were clinically depressed as measured by the Center for Epidemiologic Studies Depression Scale, and 18 percent were considered severly psychoneurotic. In their lifetimes victims were more likely than nonvictims to have had problems with depression, alcohol and other drug abuse, panic, and obsessive-compulsive symptoms (George and Winfield-Laird, 1986). In addition, a strong correlation between a history of violent victimization and suicidal ideation or deliberate attempts at self-harm has been reported (Kilpatrick, et al., 1985; Kilpatrick, et al., 1987).

With respect to the behavioral impact of abductions and sexual abuse, children and adolescents try to escape their abductor/abuser. However, their attempts are frequently met with increased violence and the threat of death, blame for the victimization, or death of their family members should they attempt to flee again. In fact, homicide is currently one of the five leading causes of child mortality in the United States (Goetting, 1990).

Another common response to children's attempts to flee is that the abductor tells the child that his or her parents do not love them or want them to come home. This strategy was used in 1972 by Kenneth Parnell when he abducted Steven Stayner. Parnell and an accomplice initially told Steven they were going to drive him home and ask his mother to make a church donation. Using this pretext, they got Steven into the car. Parnell frequently got out of the car and pretended to phone Steven's mother; he told Steven he had gotten her permission to keep Steven overnight. After learning that Steven had been punished recently by his father, Parnell played on this fact, telling Steven that his parents did not want him.

The victimized child is initially dependent upon the abductor for whatever reality is assigned to the experience (Summit, 1983). A sense of learned helplessness frequently follows such controlling statements—that no matter what they try to do, the victimization will not cease. Steven Staynor once stated, "I had hopes someday my parents would want me back . . . I used to have fantasy thoughts of family life, but as time went on they dimmed and dimmed."

Many children and adolescents respond to victimization by developing a dissociative disorder. A dissociative disorder includes various forms of memory loss and splitting of mind and body. The more serious the victimization and the longer it continues, the more likely the victim has learned how to dissociate as a psychological protection. Walker (1992) reported that in young children, especially those under five, multiple personalities may develop from the dissociation. In addition, a child may become preverbal, and if not permitted to express feelings related to the trauma, the child may continue in a chronic shock state (Bryant, 1992).

Jeanne Hernandez, in her 1992 presentation to the annual meeting of the Society of Behavioral Medicine, reported that in her study of 6,224 ninth-, and twelfth-grade students in public schools in Minnesota, physically and sexually abused boys and girls reported eating disorders, especially bulimia. The abused adolescents with eating disorders reported lower self-esteem and more stress, anxiety, hopelessness, and suicide ideation than did their peers who were not abused.

Shame is a common response by children to sexual abuse. They develop a self-image of being dirty or ruined. Children may label a male abuser's ejaculation as "peeing on me," an act children typically view as "dirty." This feeling of shame often interferes with seeking help or telling anyone about the abuse, because they fear other people will also think they are dirty and respond to them with disgust (Carlson and Quina, 1989).

In recent years, mental health professionals have recognized that psychological symptoms that result from victimization are different from those from other mental disorders (Eth and Pynoos, 1985; Rosewater, 1987; Terr, 1990). The 1980 edition of the *Diagnostic and Statistical Manual of Mental Disorders* of the American Psychiatric Association for the first time included a diagnostic category of post traumatic stress disorder (PTSD), a commonly seen psychological reaction to trauma. The features of a PTSD diagnosis include reexperiencing the traumatic events through flashbacks, nightmares, exaggerated startle response; hypervigilance to cues of further dangers; and disturbances in personal relationships. Abducted and abused children are at a nearly fourfold increased lifetime risk for any psychiatric disorder and at a threefold risk for substance abuse (Scott, 1992).

Research has suggested that abducted children who are found and returned to their families often remain psychologically tied to their abductors and continue to show psychological impairment. Steven Staynor reflected on this issue after he was returned to his family eight years after his abduction. He stated: "I returned almost a grown man, and yet my parents saw me at first as their seven-year-old. . . . Everything has changed. . . ." (quoted in Gelman, 1984, p. 82).

The age of the child must be considered as an important factor in the nature and severity of injuries resulting from victimization. For example, there is a greater vulnerability of small children to death and serious harm as a result of inflicted blows. In addition, there is a higher likelihood for older children and adolescents to contact sexual-abuse-related HIV infection, since older children suffer more penetrative sexual abuse (Kerns and Ritter, 1991).

Thus, there are severe aftereffects of an abduction that continue into the individual's adult life. These aftereffects are seen in the child's and then later the adult's health, emotional, and spiritual development, as well as what Alice Miller (1981) has termed "soul murder" or the killing of feelings.

MYTH: IT IS ONLY YOUNG, HELPLESS CHILDREN WHO ARE THE PREY OF ABDUCTORS

In 1984, executive law in New York State created the Missing Children Register, which is maintained by the New York State Division of Criminal Justice Services. In 1992, a total of 27,553 cases of missing children were reported in New York State through this register. This represented an increase of 6 percent over 1991. Of the individuals reported missing 88 percent were thirteen or older. There have even been reported cases of abductions of young women and men in their early and mid-twenties. One case that received a great deal of attention concerned the abduction of Karen Wilson, a twenty-one-year-old legislative intern at the capitol in New York State during the 1986 session, who is still missing. The single largest group of cases in 1992 in New York State involved white girls aged thirteen to fifteen. This statistic is common in other states as well.

David Finkelhor and Jennifer Dziuba-Leatherman (1994) presented the national statistics taken from several sources in order of magnitude of victimizations of children. The forms of victimization are those for which there were scientifically defensible national estimates. According to the 1990 National Crime Survey (Bureau of Justice Statistics, 1991), the rates of assault, rape, and robbery against twelve to nineteen year olds are two to three times higher than for the adult population as a whole. Finkelhor and Dziuba-Leatherman's statistics help illustrate the diversity and frequency of children's victimizations. As the researchers stated, "Almost all the figures . . . have been promoted in isolation at one time or another. Viewed together, they are just part of a total environment of various victimization dangers with which children live" (176).

Why are abductions of children more common than those of adults? While there are no easy answers to this question, there have been some generalizations reported. For example, the weakness and small physical stature of most children put them at greater risk for victimization. Children are not able to retaliate or deter violence and victimization as perhaps those with more power and strength. In addition, the social tolerance of childhood violence and victimization plays an important role. Many of the crimes against children are considered outside the purview of the criminal-justice system. For example, law enforcement officials lack the authority to rescue sixteen and seventeen year olds from street culture and assist them in obtaining needed psychological and medical care. This situation relates to the issue of persons-in-need-of-supervision (PINS). PINS are individuals under sixteen, who do not attend school as required by law, or who are incorrigible. It is important to expand our definition of someone who is likely to be abducted and abused to include these adolescents. Legislation has been introduced and is now awaiting passage in the New York State legislature to expand the age of PINS to eighteen. This issue will be addressed in chapter 7 when we discuss legislation throughout the United States.

Another reason why children are at high risk for violence and victimization is that they have comparatively little choice with whom they associate. Consequently, they may be with high-risk offenders and at jeopardy for victimization. Thus, a child who lives with a custodial parent is not free or able to leave. A child is obliged to live with other people and to go to school with other people—in what Finkelhor and Dziuba-Leatherman (1994) describe as high density, heterogenous environments.

All of these examples suggest a frightening fact that children know all too well: Children do not always have access to people and organizations in their culture that help protect them from violent people and victimization.

MYTH: RUNAWAY CHILDREN AND ADOLESCENTS ARE NOT TARGETED FOR ABDUCTIONS

The absence of choice that children have who are in violent situations is no different for runaway teens, despite the myth that adolescents are immune from abductions and other sexual violence because they left their homes by their own volition. Runaway teens are also dependent on others for survival; they are not able, for the most part, to take care of themselves. Thus, adolescents are also socially and psychologically immature, as are children.

Dependency and immaturity are used by abductors to get teens to become part of the street culture. The adolescents may engage in criminal activity to avoid being victimized by abductors, or they may engage in pornography or prostitution or take drugs as part of the abductor/abuser's "hold" on them. Other criminal activities in which runaway adolescents engage include shoplifting, robbery, and larceny.

While the illusion is that in most cases adolescents who run away from home are "acting out," or are rebelling against parents, the reality is that these teens in many instances are sexually and physically abused by family members (Silbert and Pines, 1981). Thus, adolescents' running away may be an escape attempt, not a rebellious gesture. Should they encounter an abductor/abuser, the impact of further victimization is devastating. Furthermore, there is research evidence that suggests that a history of repeated victimizations increases the likelihood that an individual will also eventually become a perpetrator of crime, violence, and/ or abuse (Hanson and Slater, 1988; Windom, 1989). Many abductors use runaway teens as accomplices to their own crimes.

MYTH: PARENTAL ABDUCTION IS NOT A SERIOUS MATTER AND IS NOT A FORM OF CHILD ABUSE

Noncustodial parent abductions account for a large percentage of the total statistics regarding missing children. Edward Goldfader of Tracers Company of America, a professional searching organization, estimates the number to be as high as 95 percent.

In some cases, noncustodial fathers are not allowed by their exwives to see their children, despite the fact that the court has granted them visitation rights. Thus, the child is sometimes used as a pawn between the parents in marital or divorce disputes. Children abducted by noncustodial parents suffer considerable psychological and emotional distress. In some cases, the children may even be further victimized by sexual or physical abuse.

Children who are abducted by noncustodial parents, similar to those abducted by strangers, lose trust in their world and feel emotionally abandoned by the adults—their parents— who are most important to their protection and recovery. They are also driven further into regression, alienation, powerlessness, shame, embarassment, humiliation, self-blame, and self-hate (Bryant, 1992).

Incestuous relationships between the noncustodial parent and the child may occur. Children are thus further manipulated into silence—about the abduction and then about the sexual abuse. As Christine Courtois (1988) stated:

> The child is manipulated by the unequal power in the relationship, that is, by the relationship with the perpetrator on whom [they] are dependent. The child is further coerced by the perpetrator's strong desire to keep the activity a secret, which has the purpose of minimizing intervention and allowing repetition. (6)

If boys and girls do disclose information about the incestuous relationship, they are typically met with disbelief and rationalization of the perpetrator's behavior. Thus, most children do not tell.

Research does suggest that 90 percent of parents who take their own children illegally are emotionally unstable or abusive, with approximately one-half having criminal records (Huttinger, 1984). The majority of noncustodial parent abductions occur before custody has been determined. Children often live under cruel circumstances, almost parallelling the life of a fugitive, with frequent changes of residences and names. As Abrahms (1983) noted in her aptly titled book, *Children in the Crossfire,* children abducted by noncustodial parents quickly "turn into cooperative hostages. They can't bear to be punished, and ponder the consequences of resistance." Tommy, for example, was dragged to seven states and was intimidated on a daily basis. He subsequently stated:

> I told my stepmom I wanted to go back to my real mom. My stepmother told me to wait until my father came home, and then he whipped me with a belt and said he didn't want me talking about Mom. It made me scared, so I stopped. (quoted in Abrahms, 1983, 35)

We will address this issue of noncustodial parental abductions further in chapter 5.

MYTH: ABDUCTIONS DO NOT HAPPEN HERE TO THE PEOPLE I KNOW—THEY HAPPEN SOMEWHERE ELSE

Most individuals believe that child abductions could never touch their lives—that they happen to other people who live far away, but never to people like themselves. One explanation for this myth concerns the "just-world hypothesis" (Lerner, 1980). Individuals who believe in a just world believe bad things happen only to those who somehow bring on or somehow deserve the consequences of their acts. We raise our children to believe in the "golden rule": that if we are good to other people, they will treat us nicely too. Notwithstanding that in many cases this tenet is true, some people believe that if anything bad happens to an individual, then they caused or at least contributed to this bad event in their lives—"That's what you get when you hitchhike," "I was a bad son; my father had to punish me." People thus try to find a personal reason for an individual's selection as a victim of violence. Why? Because the alternative realization is frightening: "It could happen to me or to someone I love."

We want to shield ourselves from the truth that sexual victimization does not distinguish between "good" people and "bad" people and that we too could be victims of violent acts. Thus, the just-world hypothesis is a protective mechanism; it shields us from a range of fears. We have to confront the reality that we are not special; we are not protected from harm.

Children and adolescents may believe in the just-world hypothesis because of the particular stage of cognitive development in which they are operating. For example, adolescents have a belief in their own uniqueness that is expressed in a subjective story they tell themselves about their "special qualities." This subjective story is referred to by David Elkind (1967) as the "personal fable." The personal fable is frequently translated into a conviction that they are not subject to the dangers suffered by others. Consequently, adolescent boys and girls may avoid using seat belts, drive too fast, binge and purge, dispense with using contraceptives, or avoid training in issues related to child abductions and missing children—all out of the conviction that "nothing bad will happen to me; I'm special."

This egocentrism disappears when girls and boys have role-taking opportunities that will help to replace the subjective story with an objective one. Such role-taking experiences include kidnap resistance training. Families and teachers may reinforce the personal fable through the myths they cling to regarding child abductions, especially the just-world hypothesis.

Had it not been for the kidnap resistance training that twelve-year-old Rebecca Saverese received in school, Lewis Lent, Jr., might never have been captured. Rebecca used the "Run, Yell, and Tell" training she had received through the DARE classes at her school in Pittsfield, Massachusetts, to free herself from the potential abduction by a man alleged to be responsible for several abductions on the East Coast. Without this training, Rebecca might not be around today to tell her story and more children might have fallen victim to Mr. Lent's activities. We will return to this issue of training in subsequent chapters.

The just-world hypothesis and personal fable are supported by silence surrounding child abductions and sexual victimization in this culture. The silence enhances our illusion of invulnerability for nonvictims. It is because none of our children and adolescents are safe that the silence must be broken.

SUMMARY

In this chapter we have identified myths or illusions society may cling to concerning missing children and those who have been sexually abused and co-opted by abusers. These "cognitive illusions" or myths are well ingrained in our culture. Most insidious are their influences upon the self-images of the children and adolescents forced to edure abduction. These myths create levels of guilt, shame, and confusion in those abducted, their families, and their friends. They deter all of us who are caring citizens in our society from being ever vigilant to do our part to protect not only our children but all children from this devastating form of child abuse.

In the next three chapters, we present children's and adolescents' accounts of their experiences with child abductors. They break their silence. Their stories are important for those of us who are developing policies and curricula, for those who counsel victims of child abductions and sexual abuse, and for those representing children and teens in court proceedings.

REFERENCES

Abel, G. (1986). Quoted in *Family Violence and Sexual Assault Bulletin*, 1991, 7(4): 19.

Abrahms, S. (1983). *Children In the Crossfire: The Tragedy of Parental Kidnapping*. New York: Atheneum.

Beneke, T. (1982). *Men on Rape*. New York: St. Martin's.

Bureau of Justice Statistics (1992). *Criminal Victimization in the United States, 1990: A National Crime Victimization*

Survey Report (NCJ-134126). Washington, DC: U.S. Department of Justice.

Burgess, A., and L. Holmstrom. (1974). Rape: Sexual Disruption and Recovery. American *Journal of Orthopsychiatry* 49, 648.

Bryant, C. (1992). "The Victimology of Children: A Transpersonal Conceptual Treatment Model." In E. Viano (ed), *Critical Issues in Victimology: International Perpectives*. New York: Springer.

Conte, J., and L. Berliner. (1988). "The Impact of Child Sexual Abuse: Empirical Findings." In L. E. A. Walker (ed.), *Handbook on Sexual Abuse of Children*. New York: Springer.

Courtois, C. (1988). *Healing the Incest Wound: Adult Survivors in Therapy*. New York: Norton.

Doyle, J., and M. Paludi. (1995). *Sex and Gender: The Human Experience*. Dubuque: Wm. C. Brown.

Eth, S., and R. Pynoos. (1985). *Post-traumatic Stress Disorder in Children*. Washington: American Psychiatric Press.

Family Violence and Sexual Assault Bulletin (1991). "Oprah Winfrey Calls for Legislation Protecting Children," 7(4): 19.

Finkelhor, D., and A. Browne. (1988). "The Traumatogenic Effects of Child Sexual Abuse." In L. E. A. Walker (ed.), *Handbook on Sexual Abuse of Children*. New York: Springer.

Finkelhor, D., and J. Dziuba-Leatherman. (1994). "Victimization of Children." *American Psychologist* 49, 173–83.

Freeman-Longo, R., and R. Wall. (1986). "Changing a Lifetime of Sexual Crime." *Psychology Today*, (March): 58–64.

Gelman, D. (1984). "Stolen children." Newsweek, (March 19): 78–86.

Goetting, A. (1990). "Child Victims of Homicide: A Portrait of Their Killers and the Circumstances of Their Deaths." *Violence and Victims* 5, 287–96.

Hanson, R., and S. Slater. (1988). "Sexual Victimization in the History of Sexual Abusers: A Review." Annals of Sex Research 4, 485–99.

Hernandez, J. (1992). "Eating Disorders and Sexual Abuse Among Adolescents." Paper presented at the annual meeting of the Society of Behavioral Medicine, New York, NY.

Huttinger, B. (1984). *My Child Is Not Missing: A Parent's Guidebook for the Prevention and Recovery of Missing Children.* Plantation, FL: Child Safe Products.

Kilpatrick, D., C. Best, L. Veronen, A. Amick, L. Villeponteaux, and G. Ruff, (1985). "Mental Health Correlates of Criminal Victimization: A Random Community Survey." *Journal of Consulting and Clinical Psychology* 53, 866–73.

Kilpatrick, D., B. Saunders, L. Veronen, C. Best, and J. Von, (1987). "Criminal Victimization: Lifetime Prevalence, Reporting to Police, and Psychological Impact." *Crime and Delinquency* 33, 479–89.

Koss, M. P. (1990). "The women's mental health research agenda: Violence against women." *American Psychologist* 45, 374–80.

Lanning, K. (1994). "Child Molesters: A Behavioral Analysis." *School Safety* (Spring): 12–17.

Lerner, M. (1980). The Belief in a Just World. New York: Plenum.

Malamuth, N., and J. Check. (1981). "Penile Tumescence and Perceptual Responses to Rape as a Function of Victim's Perceived Reactions." *Journal of Applied Social Psychology*, 10, 528–47.

Malamuth, N., and E. Donnerstein. (1982). "The Effects of Aggressive-Pornographic Mass Media Stimuli. "In L. Berkowitz (ed.), *Advances in Experimental Social Psychology.* Vol. 15 New York: Academic Press.

Quina, K., and N. Carlson. (1989). *Rape, Incest, and Sexual Harassment: A Guide for Helping Survivors.* New York: Praeger.

Rosenfeld, A. (1985). Discovering and dealing with deviant sex. *Psychology Today* (April): 8–10.

Rosewater, L. B. (1987). "A Critical Analysis of the Proposed Self-Defeating Personality Disorder." *Journal of Personality Disorders* 1, 190–95.

Russell, D. (1973). "Rape and the masculine mystique." Paper presented at the American Sociological Association, New York, NY.

Salasin, S. (ed.), (1981). *Evaluating Victim Services.* Vol. 7. Beverly Hills, CA: Sage.

Scott, K. (1992). "Childhood Sexual Abuse: Impact on a Community's Mental Health Status." *Child Abuse and Neglect* 16, 285–95.

Silbert, M., and A. Pines. (1981). "Sexual Abuse as an Antecedent to Prostitution." *Child Abuse and Neglect 5,* 407–11.

Summitt, R. (1983). *The Child Sexual Abuse Accomodation Syndrome.* Torrance, CA: Community Consultation Service, Harbor-UCLA Medical Center.

Terr, L. (1990). *Too Scared to Cry.* New York: Harper/Collins.

Walker, L. E. A. (1992). "Traumatized Populations: Role and Responsibilities of Professionals." In E. Viano (ed.), *Critical Issues in Victimology: International Perspectives.* New York: Springer.

Widom, C. S. (1989). "Does Violence Beget Violence? A Critical Examination of the Literature." *Psychological Bulletin* 106, 3–28.

Part Two

"Missing" Children and Adolescents

▮▮2

Runaways

INTRODUCTION

During the course of the writing of this chapter the authors frequently heard a commercial for an oil filter company that incorporated the slogan "Pay now or pay later" in its advertisements. The company's goal in using the phrase repeatedly throughout the commercial was to help the listener realize that future performance of automobiles was directly related to the investment made in them in the present; that time (and money) spent *now* would be a way to guarantee no or few problems in the *future*.

This sentiment is not one that most individuals cling to when it comes to taking care of their health, career development, or their safety at home or on the streets. In fact, understanding the phrase *pay now or pay later* may not even be within the grasp of most children and adolescents.

Many adolescents would not accept the idea of pay now or pay later. For them, it is the immediate present, the *now* that matters. They rarely consider how their behavior in the present could be beneficial or harmful to them in the future. They rely on what psychologist David Elkind (1967) has referred to as the "personal fable." Absorbed with their own feelings, adolescents believe their emotions are unique. This uniqueness is expressed in a subjective story they tell themselves about their "special qualities." This personal fable is frequently translated into a conviction that they are not subject to the dangers suffered by others. Consequently, they may avoid using seatbelts, dispense with using contraceptives, or run away from home—all out of the conviction that "nothing bad will happen to me—I'm special."

This egocentrism that characterizes much of adolescents' thinking skills and reasoning abilities also gets expressed in their ability to mentally compare themselves—their facial features, weight, height, muscle build—to others and to mentally compare their parents and siblings to other, perhaps more "utopian" family constellations. In fact, some adolescents develop rather elaborate stories about their being adopted—that they are really the daughter or son of much more interesting, attractive, intelligent parents who were unable to care for them due to their being missionaries or some other good reason! While the ability to think abstractly and hypothetically is a positive aspect, there is also a danger attached to these abilities. One of the negative aspects of adolescents' newly found reasoning abilities is a preoccupation with finding something better, something more interesting, something more exciting.

Unfortunately, the media—in all forms ranging from books geared for teens to after-school television programs—may reinforce adolescents' personal fables and egocentrism through romanticizing travel, independence from one's family, life on the streets, and fairy tale, glamorous relationships. Consequently, adolescents may decide to leave home in pursuit of a more exciting life as portrayed in these stories and programs. They perceive running away as a solution to problems with their parents, boyfriends or girlfriends, and peer group. They run away from their families with the conviction "I'll show them—they can't treat me like that—I'll leave." They may be seriously harming themselves in their struggle to find their identity. They also may believe that they will return home when their parents come find them and vow to treat them differently.

The fact is that the street culture for adolescents who run away from home is typically not an improvement over their own experiences with their parents and siblings (although it may be perceived as better by some adolescents who were abused at home). Running away is not a solution; it's a problem. Adolescents who become part of the street culture tend to get involved with prostitution, drug use and selling, and pornography. Adolescents are thus controlled by adults. The majority of adolescents who run away from home are never found.

In this chapter we will discuss abductions and abuse of runaway adolescents. We will also address the fact that many adolescents who run away from home are leaving because of abusive relationships. The main goal of this chapter is similar to the sentiment expressed in the advertisment for the automobile company previously mentioned: Unless we focus on the present and educate teens, parents, and the media about the realities of street culture—not the "romance" of it all, we as a society will pay in terms of the loss of our childrens' innocence, ability to trust, and, perhaps, lives. We also will pay later in terms of our own lives when runaways commit crimes to satisfy their abductor/abusers' requests, not to mention the financial toll to taxpayers through the cost of law enforcement, our judicial system, and rehabilitation for children.

An ounce of prevention must be taken with our adolescents—especially in helping them to cope with their newfound reasoning skills. We also must make an effort to get adolescents off of the streets before their lives are lost to the street culture. We must do this so we do not continue to perpetuate Joseph Epstein's sentiment, that "in a secular age, children have become the last sacred objects."

ADOLESCENCE: TRANSITION TO ADULTHOOD

Adolescence is a developmental transition between childhood and adulthood. This period is characterized by rapid physical changes, significant conceptual maturation, and heightened sensitivity to peer approval. In addition, adolescence is marked by conflict with parents (Eccles et al., 1993). As psychologist Elizabeth Douvan and her colleagues have asserted (1969), the adolescent "must continue to be a son or daughter and meet the obligations this role imposes, while at the same time abandoning the role of dependent child and gradually assuming the position of independent autonomous adult" (132).

Adolescents' efforts to adjust to their changing bodies, reasoning capabilities, and independence usher in a period of stress (Eccles et al., 1993). The stressfulness of this transitional period may be exascerbated by parental expectations to succeed, academic pressure, family conflict, separation, and divorce. Psychologist David Elkind, in *The Hurried Child* (1988), has noted that today's pressures on children to grow up fast have resulted in "miniature adults." Elkind cites as causes of stress the fashion industry, with its emphasis on adolescents dressing in provacative clothing, and attorneys encouraging children to sue their parents for a variety of grievances. Elkind also offers some insight as to the role the media plays in pressuring adolescents to grow up too soon too fast:

> The media . . . , including music, books, films, and television, increasingly portray young people as precocious and present them in more or less explicit sexual or manipulative situations. Such portrayals force children to think they should act grown up before they are ready. . . . The media promote not only teenage sexuality but also the wearing of adult clothes and the use of adult behaviors, language, and interpersonal strategies. Sexual promotion occurs in the context of other suggestions and models for growing up fast. (11)

Despite adolescents' adopting adult clothing, sexual situations, and other behaviors, adolescents don't feel like adults. As Elkind (1988) pointed out, "Growing up emotionally is complicated and difficult under any circumstances but may be especially so when children's behavior and appearance speak 'adult' while their feelings cry 'child' " (12).

The normative experience of physical and cognitive development not occuring simultaneously with emotional development becomes problematic for some teens. Pushed to grow up fast by the media, their peer group, and some parents, adolescents suddenly find themselves being denied many adult prerogatives they assumed would be their prerogatives, such as smoking, drinking, and driving. These experiences are denied them until they reach a certain age. Thus, many adolescents feel betrayed by their families and other adults who encouraged them to grow up fast but at the same time force them to remain children. The storm and stress of growing up fast result in troubled and troublesome behavior during the adolescent period.

Adolescents may rush to experiment with alcohol or other drugs and sexual behavior. Adolescents often turn to drugs and sexual behavior as short-cut answers. They endanger their physical and psychological health in the process and leave their problems unsolved (Papalia and Olds, 1990). Patterns of drug use among adolescents follow those among adults: adolescents take stimulants and barbiturates to alleviate unhappiness, depression, and day-to-day pressures. Adolescents report that they begin drinking because it seems like a grown up thing to do. They continue to drink for the same reasons as adults—to be accepted by peers, to reduce anxiety, and to escape from problems. Surveys of high school adolescents conducted by the National Institute on Drug Abuse show that there is a high proportion of adolescents who are problem drinkers. More than three out of ten had been intoxicated at least four times or had gotten into trouble with the school administration, peers, or the police because of drinking at least twice in the previous year. The leading cause of death among fifteen- to twenty-four-year-old Americans is alcohol-related motor vehicle accidents (Johnston, O'Malley, and Bachman, 1988).

Other adolescent responses to the stress of growing up too fast are crime and violence. Adolescents are attacked in high school, and many miss school because they are afraid they will be attacked. Even school teachers are physically attacked, and a large proportion of adolescents carry weapons to school. Reporter Lisa Austin, offered the following examples (1987):

> On a Texas playground, a 14-year old wounded a classmate, then told the principal, "That was the only way I could get him off my back, Mr. Brown."

> A Montana 14-year-old killed a teacher. He said his failure in French class prompted the shooting.

Donna Mates and Kenneth Allison (1992) facilitated a series of focus-group interviews with tenth-grade students in three high schools in Toronto, Ontario. The focus groups were used to identify major sources of stress and coping responses of adolescents. The following sources of stress were discussed by the adolescents: parents/family, work/money, friends, addictions/drugs, and gangs/strangers. The students reported conflict with their parents regarding what they were going to do with their future, the importance of good grades, and parents' inability to listen to what their son/daughter was saying to them. The adolescents frequently remarked on problems with parental control—that they were forced to do certain things and not permitted to do others. With respect to adolescent girls, Mates and Allison reported that they listed problems such as parental dissatisfaction with boyfriends, strict rules, lack of parental trust, and problems related to their parents' opinions concerning dress and the use of cosmetics.

In adolescents' own voices:

> You are old enough to know that; you're too young to do that—well, what are you?

> When you act older, they tell you to act younger.

> And they bring up all this stuff to make you feel guilty for what you are old enough to do. (466)

By drug use, sexual behavior, and violence, adolescents are trying to shed the identity of their parents' children and establish their own separate identities. Parents may want to enforce more control over their adolescents so they can conform to social rules. This may be accomplished by demanding stricter curfews, refusal to purchase certain articles of clothing, or prohibition against seeing some members of their peer group. While most parents and adolescents can resolve their disagreements to everybody's satisfaction, in some situations, adolescents want to escape their parents' control and influence. One way to cope with the pressures of home life is running away from home. These adolescents believe running away will prove a point to the parents—that they will lose their child unless they change their ways. Rarely, however, does this strategy work. It's never well conceptualized; it is usually based on unrealistic, romantic ideas about surviving on one's own and ignores the reality of street culture.

THE PROCESS OF RUNNING AWAY

Most adults don't espouse the "pay now or pay later" concept when it comes to understanding the seriousness of adolescent runaways—an issue that must be addressed by parents, teachers, and lawmakers. The fact is that the majority of missing children—more than 1 million each year nationally—are adolescent runaways. According to the New York State 1992 Missing Children Register, the vast majority of missing children cases involved suspected runaways (91 percent). Palenski and Launer (1987) identified running away as a process with several steps: family disengagement, effects of friends as role models, recognizing the "right" situation, shrinking alternatives, and managing the residuals. We will summarize each of the stages in this process.

Family Disengagement

The major factor in the process of deciding to run away from home is family disengagement. Adolescents who have run away from home have reported that prior to leaving home, they felt their involvement with their families was at minimum. The everyday routine of being family members, being interested, responsible, or accountable to parents, was no longer important to them (Palenski and Launer, 1987). As adolescents interviewed by Joseph Palenski and Harold Launer (1987) stated: "I found myself slowly being left out. If you can't talk to anybody, you're left out." and "After a while, I just listened and didn't say anything. I figured, why bother" (351).

Effects of Friends as Role Models

As adolescents' family involvement becomes less frequent, other influences become more attractive. They frequently see some friends respond to similar problems with parents by leaving the situation, by running away from home. Adolescents in research by Palenski and Launer (1987) stated that running away was not perceived as a possiblity until they saw others with similar problems leave home. Thus, friends may serve as role models or mentors for adolescents by instructing them in how to leave home. Unfortunately, these models or mentors confirm adolescents' feelings that everything will be fine once they leave their home for a while.

Recognizing the Right Situation

Palenski and Launer (1987) reported that adolescents who run away from home decide to do so when they are either in a state of extreme turmoil or in one of extreme passivity. Adolescents report their need to see their point of view of running away as a matter of "justice." Adolescents rarely leave for the sake of leaving. They run away because family life is too problematic for them.

Shrinking Alternatives

Adolescents who decide to run away from home do so when other alternatives to the problems they were having with their parents seem no longer viable. For example, if the problems the adolescent was facing did not necessitate bringing in law enforcement officials, physicians, or some other authority, an alternative to running away was possible. However, once a third party becomes involved in the situation, adolescents believe that the best way to protect themselves is to flee the situation.

Managing the Residuals

Palenski and Launer reported that adolescents who had decided to run away from home had some misgivings about their behavior. For example: "I was glad I left, but not so glad about staying away. You know, like it was different" (355).

Runaways have to consider attending school, clothing, shelter, and food—basic survival. If they attend a runaway program, such as Covenant House in New York City, they will get assistance with these residuals of running away. However, less fortunate adolescents receive help with the residuals from abductors and abusers they encounter once they are part of the street culture.

TERRIFIED RUNNERS: VICTIMS OF INCEST

Some runaways leave home due to conflict with parents, and some may be attracted to the excitement offered by a street subculture. However, research has also documented that some adolescents run away from home as a desperate escape attempt from emotionally, physically, and sexually abusive homes, what Greene and Esselstyn (1972) call "terrified runners."

Adolescents and children suffer sexual and physical abuse from family members and adult family friends at an alarming rate (Finkelhor and Dziuba-Leatherman, 1994). In nearly one-third of all sex crimes reported to the police, the victims are under fourteen (Quina and Carlson, 1989). One physician stated that in his experience, sexual abuse of children and adolescents is "more common . . . than broken bones and tonsillectomies" (Green, quoted in Rush, 1980, 5). Estimates between 75 percent and 95 percent have been reported for the incidence of childhood sexual and physical assaults. At least 10 percent of girls and 5 percent of boys are victims of incest.

Incest is illegal throughout the United States, but the laws vary by state as to the behavior and degree of relatedness considered incestuous. Incest refers to sexual contact between a child/adolescent and a person considered an ineligible partner because of blood and/or social ties to the child/adolescent's family (e.g., mother, father, stepparent, grandparent, uncle, aunt, sibling, in-laws). The percentages of incest victims translate into 100,000 children who are molested each year (Finkelhor and Dziuba-Leatherman, 1994). While the illusion is that incest occurs more often in families of working-class background, in racial minority families, and in rural families, these beliefs have not been substantiated by research (Russell, 1984).

Boys and girls who are victims of incest suffer aftereffects, in many cases serious enough to warrant therapy in adulthood (Terr, 1990). Sexually victimized children appear to be at a nearly fourfold increased lifetime risk for any psychiatric disorder and at a threefold risk for substance abuse (Saunders et al., 1992; Scott, 1992). In fact, Scott (1992) estimated that approximately 8 percent of all psychiatric cases within the population at large can be attributed to childhood sexual assault.

Reports of survivors of incestuous relationships indicate that adolescents inflict serious physical harm on themselves, either directly through self-mutiliation or indirectly through eating disorders or medical neglect. Survivors may also attempt suicide. These responses provide evidence that sexual abuse creates a serious potential for self-destructive behaviors.

REALITIES OF STREET LIFE FOR RUNAWAY ADOLESCENTS

While the majority of adolescents who decide to run away from home have thought through their decision to leave—whether for reasons of safety from sexual abuse or from conflicts with parents—they have not clearly thought through what will happen to them once they are part of the street culture. Palenski and Launer (1987) reported that the majority of runaway adolescents they interviewed were not sure of themselves, especially as to what they were going to do to support themselves.

Thus, what first may seem to be a solution to their problems or a weapon designed to alter their parents' discipline becomes an intolerable burden. Runaway teens are not prepared for the callousness and indifference of individuals they encounter on the street, let alone the cruelty of some individuals who are waiting for the opportunity to abuse them even more. Some adolescents who believe they are grown up and can enter the world of adults without punishment from parents frequent bars and adult movie houses where they encounter abusers or abductors. These adolescents as well as those who appear alone and frightened are easily spotted and are quickly identified as "the new kids" (Huttinger, 1984).

The immediate needs of runaway adolescents are safety and shelter, and often medical attention or treatment for drug or alcohol abuse. Frequently, they are offered these necessities by abductors. Research has also suggested that some runaways are encouraged to engage in these behaviors by their abductors as a way of preventing effective protest (Quina and Carlson, 1989). Following a con attack (see chapter 1), abductors are able to manipulate runaway teens into prostitution, pornography, or drug selling. In many instances, abductors force adolescents into perpetrating violent crimes against innocent victims for monetary gain. For the terrified runners who have experienced sexual abuse at home, by the time they reach the street, their bodies and emotional health have been so objectified and degraded that prostitution, pornography, or drug abuse does not seem shocking or foreign (Quina and Carlson, 1989). In some cities, child prostitution and child pornography are controlled. Huttinger (1984) noted that "local and national call services and 'buy-a-kid' rings sell runaway children for a night or permanently. The cost of buying a child for life can run from $500 to $5,000" (112). Thus, runaway adolescents are the most vulnerable people to further abuse.

Furthermore, because runaway adolescents have no health insurance nor access to medical care, disease is quite common. With the high rates of AIDS among adolescent prostitutes, the possibility of HIV infection must also be considered. In fact, runaway adolescents are considered to be in the highest risk groups for HIV infection (along with homosexual, intravenous drug users, and the homeless) (Millstein, 1989).

Added to the risk of HIV transmission among adolescents through unprotected sexual activity and IV drug use and/or sexual relations with IV drug users, is the misunderstanding of the causes, prevention, and treatment of the AIDS virus (DiClemente, Boyer, and Morales, 1988). Their personal fable about being unique is supported by the often long latency between HIV transmission and the emergence of AIDS symptoms, a period lasting eight to ten years.

Runaway adolescents' experiences as part of the street culture are nothing like the idealized version they thought they would be. The absence of choice that children have who are in violent situations is no different for runaway teens, despite the myth that adolescents are immune from abductions and other sexual violence because they left home of their own volition (see chapter 1). Runaway teens are dependent on others for survival; they are not able, for the most part, to take care of themselves.

Dependency and immaturity are used by abductors to lure teens into the street culture. The adolescents may engage in criminal activity to avoid being victimized by an abductor, or they may engage in pornography, prostitution, or drug use as part of the abductor/abuser's hold on them. Other criminal activities in which runaway adolescents engage include robbery and larceny.

Research suggests that a history of repeated victimizations increases the likelihood that an individual will eventually become a perpetrator of crime, violence, or self-abuse (Hanson and Slater, 1988; Windom, 1989). Many abductors use runaway teens as accomplices to their own crimes.

Runaways face poverty, hunger, exploitation, and murder. Rarely are they found and returned to their families. However, when a runaway adolescent is located, the current laws create a legal "catch 22" that makes it very difficult to return the teens who do not want to be returned to their families.

Section 1012 of the Family Court Act provides that a child under eighteen must be provided with shelter by the parents. Under Section 718-A of the Family Court Act, however, only a boy under sixteen or a girl under eighteen must be returned home. This discrepancy in law makes it possible for parents with runaway adolescents between sixteen and eighteen to be petitioned by Family Court to provide their children with necessities, yet have no authority to bring their children back home. There is thus an urgent need for consistency in treatment of runaway teens, an issue to which we will return in part three of this book.

SUMMARY

In this chapter we have provided an overview of the issues unique to the adolescent stage of the life cycle that contribute to teens' questioning their own identity as part of a family constellation. These issues were addressed in the context of Elkind's theory of "hurried adolescents." We also addressed ways adolescents cope with the stress of "hurrying," one of which is running away from home. A discussion of the process of running away was presented, including the realities of street culture for runaways.

Throughout the research and theory presented in this chapter is a plea for parents, teachers, and concerned adults in adolescents' lives to encourage teens' growth, learning, and questioning. There is a need to recognize the special state of adolescents to follow child development expert Penelope Leach's (1994) advice and put children and adolescents at the center of society, that is, put them *first*:

> We need to remind ourselves that . . . children require in-
> tensive, personalized, and long-lasting care. . . . It takes
> people at least five further years of physical growth and
> intellectual and social maturation to refine those skills so
> that adolescents can begin to function as adults within the
> value system of their particular culture. (xv)

Leach points out that children and adolescents will only come first in society if parents will start them as "first in their own lives without condemning themselves to coming last" (261). Elkind (1988) shares Leach's sentiment:

> If we can overcome some of the stresses of our adult lives
> and decenter, we can begin to appreciate the value of child-
> hood with its own special joys, sorrows, worries, and re-
> wards. Valuing childhood . . . means . . . seeing it as an
> important period of life to which children are entitled. (202)

When adolescents run away from us and become part of the street culture, we all suffer. We become fearful for our own lives and the lives of our loved ones. We suffer economically for the legal costs of attorneys, judges, law-enforcement personnel and institutional support. By putting children first, by giving social and economic priority to children's well-being, development, and education *now*, we will protect the *future* of childhood and adolescence, as well as adulthood. The company whose advertisements we still see seems to have provided us with an important lesson. We as a society must pay now or through the lost lives of our children we will surely pay to a larger extent in the future.

REFERENCES

Austin, L. (1987). "Student Shooting on the Rise." *The Wichita Eagle Beacon* (March 15).

DiClemente, R., C. Boyer, and E. Morales. (1988). "Minorities and AIDS: Knowledge, Attitude, and Misconceptions Among Black and Latino Adolescents." *American Journal of Public Health* 78, 55–57.

Eccles, J., C. Midgley, A. Wigfield, C. Buchanan, D. Reuman, C. Flanagan, and D. Mac Iver. (1993). "Development during Adolescence." *American Psychologist* 48, 90–101.

Elkind, D. (1967). "Egocentrism in Adolescence." *Child Development* 38, 1025–34.

———. (1988). *The Hurried Child: Growing Up Too Fast Too Soon.* New York: Addison-Wesley.

Finkelhor, D., and J. Dziuba-Leatherman (1994). "Victimization of Children." *American Psychologist* 49, 173–83.

Gold, M., and E. Douvan. (1969). *Adolescent Development: Readings in Research and Theory.* Boston: Allyn & Bacon.

Greene, N., and T. Esselstyn. (1972). "The Beyond-Control Girl." *Juvenile Justice* 23, 13–19.

Hanson, R., & S. Slater. (1988). "Sexual Victimization in the History of Sexual Abusers: A Review." *Annals of Sex Research* 4, 485–99.

Huttinger, B. (1984). *My Child Is Not Missing: A Parents' Guidebook for the Prevention and Recovery of Missing Children.* Plantation, FL: Ratzlaff & Wright Associates.

Johnston, L., P. O'Malley, and J. Bachman. (1988). *National Trends in Drug Use and Related Factors among American High School Students and Young Adults. National trends through 1987.* Rockville, MD: National Institute on Drug Abuse.

Leach, P. (1994). *Children First: What Our Society Must Do and Is Not Doing for Our Children Today.* New York: Knopf.

Mates, D., and K. Allison. (1992). "Sources of Stress and Coping Responses of High School Students." *Adolescence* 27, 461–75.

Millstein, S. (1989). *Behavioral Risk Factors for AIDS among Adolescents.* Paper presented at the annual meeting of the Society for Research in Child Development, Kansas City, MO.

Palenski, J., and H. Launer. (1987). "The 'Process' of Running Away: A Redefinition." *Adolescence* 22, 347–62.

Papalia, D., and S. W. Olds. (1990). *A Child's World: Infancy through Adolescence.* New York: McGraw-Hill.

Quina, K., and N. Carlson. (1989). *Rape, Incest, and Sexual Harassment: A Guide for Helping Survivors.* New York: Praeger.

Rush, F. (1980). *The Best Kept Secret: Sexual Abuse of Children.* Englewood Cliffs, NJ: Prentice Hall.

Russell, D. (1984). *Sexual Exploitation, Rape, Child Sexual Abuse and Workplace Harassment.* Beverly Hills, CA: Sage.

Saunders, B. E., L. Villeponteaux, J. Lipovsky, D. Kilpatrick, and L. Veronen. (1992). "Child Sexual Assault as a Risk Factor for Mental Disorders among Women: A Community Survey." *Journal of Interpersonal Violence* 7, 189–204.

Scott, K. D. (1992). "Childhood Sexual Abuse: Impact on a Community's Mental Health Status." *Child Abuse and Neglect* 16, 285–95.

Terr, L. (1990). *Too Scared to Cry.* New York: Harper/Collins.

Widom, C. S. (1989). "Does Violence Beget Violence? A Critical Examination of the Literature." *Psychological Bulletin* 106, 3-28.

|||3

Stranger Abductions

INTRODUCTION

The authors recently had an opportunity to visit a bookstore and heard a mother reading the fairy tale, *Little Red Riding Hood* to three children who appeared engrossed in every word of the story. As we listened to the tale we began to "hear" it in a different way—not the words of the tale per se, but the hidden messages the tale was imparting to children. In short, we perceived the tale as directing children—perhaps girls in particular—to handle themselves with strangers (identified as the wolf) in ways that are counterproductive to their safety from stranger abductions. According to the tale (different adaptations exist, but all convey the identical message):

> Now the wolf, as you probably know, was a wicked animal, and not to be trusted. But he was very polite when he spoke to Little Red Riding Hood.
>
> "Where are you going, little girl?" the wolf asked.
>
> "To Grandmother's house," she said. "I am taking this basket of food to her because she is sick." She happily answered all his questions. She even told him where her grandmother lived and how to get there!
>
> While she chatted, that wicked wolf was thinking about how much he'd like to eat Little Red Riding Hood and her basket of food. . . .
>
> The wolf, wanting only to eat tender Little Red Riding Hood, rolled the poor old woman under the bed. Then he disguised himself with her lacy cap and nightgown and jumped into her bed. And there he waited. . . .

43

And forever after, Little Red Riding Hood always obeyed her mother and never left the path when she walked in the woods. (1993 by Publications International)

These passages—and the rest of the tale—illustrate that (1) girls will be rewarded if they demonstrate passivity, obedience, and submissiveness; (2) men are aggressive and shrewd; (3) magic and miracles are the means by which social problems are resolved; and (4) girls are naive, negligent, and responsible for their sexual violation. All four of these hidden messages relate to the stereotypes we discussed in chapter 1 regarding stranger abductions and responses to a potential abductor.

Research and experience suggest that children must be taught to value themselves and that they have rights where adults are concerned; that they have the right, for example, to fight back and not please adults if they feel frightened or uncomfortable. Rebecca Saverese received such training in her Pittsfield, Massachusetts, school district, and in putting into practice what she had been encouraged to do—"Run, Yell, and Tell"—Rebecca freed herself from the potential abduction by Lewis Lent, Jr.

By the same token, children must not be taught that they have to stay away from everyone. We must not frighten children, an issue to be addressed in more detail in part three of this book. Instead, we need to make it clear that most adults do care about children's protection and only a very small percentage of individuals hurt children.

In *Never Say Yes to a Stranger,* Susan Newman (1985) empowers children by instructing them in the following way:

> Just because a grown-up is bigger and older doesn't mean he's smarter, and it doesn't mean you have to do what he says. You're a person too. And a very important one. You have rights. You must use those rights to protect yourself. If your gut reaction—that's the feeling that comes from inside and hits you like a brick-warns you to beware, listen to it. You may not know exactly what is causing you to feel upset or why a person gives you the "creeps." But if you ever feel uneasy or think you may be in danger, forget what you were taught about being polite, being "good" and obeying adults.

Say "No" and yell for help when a stranger orders you to do anything you know is wrong. When this happens to grown-ups, they say "No" and shout, and so should you. This is not the time to be a big shot or to be quietly brave. And it is certainly not the time to be weak and wishy-washy. Don't make it easy for them. Think: No way, stranger. Not me. Give them the hardest time you can. (125–27)

In this chapter, we will discuss the current research on stranger abductions, beginning with an overview of profiles of individuals who engage in this behavior. We will also discuss common lures used by stranger abductors (see also chapter 1). According to the national Center for Missing and Exploited Children, 200 to 300 children are abducted by strangers. In addition, approximately 114,600 abductions have been attempted unsuccessfully. Though much remains to be done in terms of education and legislation, identifying these problems is the first stage in the movement toward eradication.

We, as parents, teachers, and concerned adults, must rewrite and retell the "scripts" of the fairy tales to our children in ways Susan Newman has illustrated. By retelling and rewriting the scripts we will create hope for our children. This hope includes children rejecting the suggestions found in the fairy tales and taking more control in their lives.

WHO ARE STRANGER ABDUCTORS?

According to the Behavioral Science Unit of the Federal Bureau of Investigation, the following categories of stranger abductors have been documented: pedophiles, profiteers, serial killers, and childless psychotics. We would like to provide an overview of each of these categories, noting relevant theories and research findings as well as actual cases identified by the Center for Missing and Exploited Children.

Pedophiles

Pedophiles constitute the single largest number of child abductors. According to the *Diagnostic and Statistical Manual of Mental Disorders* of the American Psychiatric Association,

pedophila is "recurrent, intense, sexual urges and sexually arous-
ing fantasies, of at least six month's duration, involving sexual
activity with a prepubescent child. The age of the child is generally 13 or younger. The age of the person is arbitrarily set at
age 16 years or older and at least five years older than the
child." Thus, a pedophile is a significantly older individual who
prefers to have sex with individuals legally considered children
and whose sexual fantasies and erotic imagery focus on children. Not all pedophiles abduct and abuse children. Pedophiles
who do abduct children may do so for a short time, or they may
try to keep the children indefinitely (Lanning, 1994).

David Greenberg and his colleagues (Greenberg,
Bradford, and Curry, 1993), in their investigation of pedophiles,
reported that the majority of pedophiles indicated that they
were molested at a younger age than individuals who had been
molested and who were not pedophiles. Furthermore, the
pedophiles reported that they choose their age-specific victims
in accordance with the age of their own experiences of sexual
victimization. Reuben Lang and Ron Langevin (1991) reported
that pedophiles, especially those who used force in their offenses, were more likely to have had significant disruptions in
father-son relationships during childhood. A similar finding
was reported by Marc Levant and Barry Bass (1991). Identification is formed with parents during early childhood. In families from which pedophiles typically come, identification does
not occur in the same manner or to the same extent. These
formative years are characterized by abuse and ineffectual
parenting and disciplining styles, anger, hostility, and parental
noninvolvement with childrearing.

Pedophiles identify with children better than with adults,
which is related to the ability to seduce children; they "understand" their needs and problems at home or in school.

Most pedophiles collect child pornography, that is, the
record of sexual abuse or exploitation of a child. The pornography is used by pedophiles for sexual arousal and gratifica-
tion and is a prelude to actual sexual activity with children. In
addition, pedophiles may use child pornography to lower
children's inhibitions, as blackmail, as a way to communicate

with other pedophiles, or for profit (Lanning, 1994), the latter being referred to as "profiteering."

Profiteers

A profiteer is an individual who is a criminal exploiter who sells children to pornographers or adoption rings. The field of child pornography has developed into a highly organized multimillion-dollar industry with operations on a nationwide scale. Some children and adolescents become involved in child pornography after running away from home (see chapter 2); however, many children are abducted by profiteers who want to use them in pornographic films or photographs (Hunt and Baird, 1990).

Individuals who abduct children instead may be selling them in black-market adoptions.

Serial Killers

Child abductors may move from state to state kidnapping and murdering their victims. Ludwig Lowenstein (1992) reviewed the literature on obsessed compulsive killers and reported that they had often suffered from depression or conduct disorders as children, and had disorders about attachment. Furthermore, serial killers express omnipotence and a reliance on fantasy. Their actions are methodical and ritualized, with power, dominance, and control as the most frequent motivational themes (Drukteinis, 1992), as evidenced in the late 1970s by John Wayne Gacy who was convicted of the murder of sixty-one children and youths in Atlanta from 1979 to 1981.

Childless Psychotics

Children may be abducted by individuals who are not able to have children of their own or have lost a child and seek another to fill the parental void. For example, Denise Kay Gravely, two years old at the time of her abduction, was taken from her own backyard by Charles Gress, who took her to the home of his mother, Mrs. Schmidt, approximately 150 miles away. Mrs. Schmidt's daughter had died at birth several years prior to this abduction, and Mrs. Schmidt continually spoke of wanting a

daughter. Her son believed he could fulfill her wish by present-
ing Denise to his mother as his own child. Denise lived away
from her family for approximately nineteen months before
Donald Gress, brother to Charles and good friend of Denise's
father, located the child at the home of his mother.

COMMON LURES USED
BY STRANGER ABDUCTORS

As we indicated in chapter 1, Burgess and Holmstrom (1974) identified two types of modus operandi that can apply to all of the
"strangers" just reviewed: the blitz attack and the confidence or
con assault. In the blitz attack, an abductor appears suddenly. In
the confidence or con assault, an elaborate scheme is set up by the
abductor/abuser. This is a psychological rather than a physical assault,
which has, as its first requirement, gaining the confidence of the
targeted child or adolescent. The target's trust is used to manipulate
her or him into physical and psychological vulnerability.

There are common methods used by stranger abductors
to reach this goal. These methods are referred to as "lures"
and include the following:

Asking for Directions

This is a frequently used lure for stranger abductors, who trick
children into believing they are friends and need their help. As
Newman and other educators point out with respect to this
lure, it is not common for adults to ask children for help.
When adults are lost, they ask other adults for directions.
Asking the way to the police station or another place that
connotes safety (e.g., hospital) is a common technique, the goal
of which is to get the child offguard.

Asking for Help to Locate a Pet

This lure works successfully most times because it is a request
that children find difficult to refuse. This request (often the
abductor shows the child a leash) is frequently accompanied
by a detour into a woody or other secluded area.

Telling the Child That a Parent Has Been in an Accident and Is Hurt

This common lure is a form of the blitz attack and thus disarms children, who want to go to their parent(s).

Knocking at a House Door/Ringing the Doorbell to Gain Entry into the House

Common illustrations of this technique include abductors showing children and/or their babysitters fake badges, identifying themselves as repair, or delivery persons, or as individuals who have been authorized to take the children to their parents, who are supposedly injured.

Offering to Give Children a Ride Home to Their Parents

Steven Stayner (see chapter 1) was told by his abductor, Kenneth Parnell, that he could get a ride home from school with him since he, Parnell, had to ask Mrs. Stayner to make a church donation. Instead of taking Steven home, Parnell pretended to phone Mrs. Stayner and then told Steven she had given Steven permission to spend the night with Parnell. During the course of their time together, Parnell learned that Steven had been punished by his father recently. He used this as a lure: he told Steven that his parents didn't want him anymore. About a week after the abduction, Parnell told Steven that he had court papers to change Steven's name to Dennis, and he requested that the boy refer to him as "Dad." It wasn't until a few years later that Steven realized that Parnell had been lying. Steven began to realize "things weren't right—my parents wouldn't have hired a guy to pick me off the street."

VULNERABLE CHILDREN

The lures used by stranger abductors are more often used with certain types of children than with others. Those children that are more vulnerable to stranger abductions are the quiet, thoughtful ones, children who appear to have special and intense needs for adult affection and approval. Other vulnerable children include those who are loners—withdrawn, with poor social skills with children their own age. Children who look unclean or unkempt, thus in need of attention, are also vulnerable to abductors. However, we should point out, that any child who has discipline problems at school or at home may be vulnerable. Also vulnerable are those involved in situations such as separation, or divorce (see chapter 4), or illness.

Relying on case histories, Beverly Huttinger (1984) outlined the following physical situations that create vulnerability for all children:

Walking alone to or from school (especially before or after normal school hours);

Waiting for a school bus alone;

Playing in a public park or playground after hours or late in the evening or playing unsupervised any time;

Exploring remote areas in buildings;

Using enclosed, poorly lit stairways, corridors, and public rooms (e.g., apartment laundries);

Riding a bicycle alone or at night;

Using late night or all night facilities, such as laundromats;

Waiting in public parking lots (e.g. at malls) after dark or in normal working hours;

Walking unattended in a crowded mall or other public place;

Wearing articles of clothing that have their name prominently displayed; thus allowing abductors to portray familiarity.

STRANGERS' EXPLANATIONS FOR THEIR ABDUCTIONS

Research has documented predictable reactions on the part of stranger abductors following the finding of the child. These responses can be categorized in the following way: denial, minimization, justification, fabrication, claiming mental illness, or pleading "guilty, but not guilty" (Lanning, 1994). We will briefly describe each of these responses.

Denial

The common first response from stranger abductors is compelete denial. They typically act surprised, shocked, and indignant about an allegation of abduction. Or they may deny the sexual component of the act and say such things as "Is it a crime to hug a child?" These expressions of denial are commonly aided by relatives, colleagues, and friends, most of whom still rely on the stereotype that abductors are pathological, sinister individuals (see chapter 1).

Minimization

If denial as a coping mechanism doesn't work because of the overwhelming evidence against them, abductors try to lessen the offense, both in quality and in quantity. For example, an abductor may claim the sexual abuse happened on one isolated occasion or that she or he only touched the child. This strategy is often aided by victims themselves who have dissociated themselves from each victimization (see chapter 1) and cope with the abuse through denial of the number of times the abuse occurred.

Justification

Abductors may characterize themselves as high-minded, nurturing individuals whose motives are misunderstood by individuals not as "moral" as they are. Recently, a justification used by abductors concerns the so-called fact that their behavior is not seen as "politically correct" and thus interpreted as wrongful. Still other abductors claim that they are under stress and thus they are not to be blamed for the abuse.

Fabrication

Lanning (1994) cited a case of a child abductor, a physician, who claimed he was doing research on male youth prostitution. Another abductor, a college professor, reported that his behavior was simply part of his research on pedophilia—that he had to collect and distribute child pornography as part of his scientific methodology. Some abductors claim they are providing sex education for the children.

Mental Illness

Usually as a last option, child abductors may claim they have a mental illness and this illness caused them to abduct and abuse children.

Guilty but Not Guilty

Abductors often try to make a deal in order to avoid a public trial. They are thus likely to plead guilty but not guilty. Occasionally this involves a plea of *nolo contendere* to avoid civil liability. Abductors may claim that they are pleading guilty because they don't want to put the children through a trial or because they have insufficient funds to cover legal expenses. Unfortunately, it is possible for an individual to plead guilty to a charge while at the same time not acknowledge that she or he committed the crime. This has some serious implications for the coping and healing the child victims must go through; they never get closure on the victimization. This guilty but not guilty plea futher confuses children as to who is guilty and who is innocent, an issue with which they deal throughout their lives (see chapter 1).

Some abductors plead guilty to charges with vague names, such as *contributing to the delinquency of a minor* or *lewd and lascivious conduct*. This procedure also does not permit the community to know what actually occurred.

PSYCHOLOGICAL FACTORS LEADING TO ABDUCTIONS

Despite the variety of responses abductors may give to explain their behavior, serious confessions by mentally competent sexual abusers reveal consistently that the majority know they have exploited a child or adolescent for entirely personal reasons (Beneke, 1982). In addition, as we pointed out in chapter 1, abductors are not motivated primarily by sexual needs. Rather, sexual satisfaction is often absent or is present only with the humiliation of the victim. It is thus inseparable from psychological needs (Quina and Carlson, 1989).

Reuben Lang and Roy Frenzel (1988) interviewed fifty-two male incest and fifty pedophillic offenders aged twenty to fifty-two about their motivations for luring children. Offenders from both categories reported using a slow "courtship" or grooming process to seduce children with gifts, attention, and affection. All participants spoke of using power, threats, and force in sexual abuse. Other studies have confirmed Lang and Frenzel's finding, that the primary goals of an abductor are the expression of anger and a feeling of power, defined in terms of dominance and humiliation. In summary, research (e.g., Greeman-Longo and Wall, 1986; Malinosky-Rummell and Hansen, 1993; Quina and Carlson, 1989; Russell, 1975) on the psychological explanations of child abductions suggest that abductors

1. express little or no concern, trust, or empathy for others, especially their victims;

2. cannot express anger in ways that are not violent, and express their anger toward children because the latter are less likely to confront their power;

3. typically view sexual victimization as an element of the masculine role in society;

4. may have been sexually abused themselves;

5. believe that the abduction does not have serious consequences for their victims;

6. are likely to be repeat offenders since the underlying psychological problems are not resolved by the abduction.

IMPACT OF ABDUCTIONS ON CHILDREN AND THEIR COMMUNITIES

We have addressed this issue in detail in chapter 1. A summary of the research in this area is provided here. While abductors typically view their behavior as harmless, the impact of the abduction and subsequent sexual and physical abuse on the children is enormous. In their recent review of the research on long-term consequences of childhood sexual and physical abuse, Robin Malinosky-Rummell and David Hansen (1993) reported that: substance abuse, self-injurious and suicidal behavior, anxiety, depression, dissociation, and academic and vocational difficulties are more likely in abused children. Kathleen Kendall-Tackett and her colleagues (Kendall-Tackett, William, and Finkelhor, 1993), in their review of forty-five studies, reported that sexually abused children have more symptoms than nonabused children. Fears, post-traumatic stress disorder, behavior problems, sexualized behaviors, and poor self-esteem occurred most frequently among a long list of symptoms noted.

Because child abduction has a radiating impact on the victims' family, friends, and neighbors, researchers Mary Peach and Dennis Klass (1987) studied the grief of parents of children who had been murdered. Reports of their one year of participant observation with a self-help group, Parents of Murdered Children, suggested that parents experience an overwhelming anger and drive for revenge, that they are unable to resolve grief until the legal process has been completed, and that they are fearful for themselves and for their other children.

The treatment approaches discussed in part three of this book address crisis intervention, advocacy, and counseling for victims and their families and members of the community. Special attention will be devoted to crisis intervention with children who were friends of the victims, for they too suffer long-term consequences of a friend's abduction and absence and subsequent death.

SUMMARY

The March 19, 1984, issue of *Newsweek* devoted its cover story to the issue of missing children with the headline "Stolen Children—What Can Be Done about Child Abductions." It has been more than ten years since this article appeared, and little has changed since then. Children are still being abducted, abused, and murdered by strangers. Most of the children's whereabouts are unknown. These are frightening realities, and states should take the window of opportunity created by the concerns about the most recent abduction tragedies and require that abduction prevention techniques be taught in schools. Parents also need to instruct children about abductions. There are countless courses for children about AIDS and how to prevent sexual abuse. Training must also empower children in confronting stranger abductors. In part three of this book we offer suggestions for meeting this goal for parents, teachers, and legislators. The real tragedy would be if the outrage felt by child victims and their families, friends, and neighbors continues to go unanswered for another ten years and we add more names to the list of children who might never be found.

REFERENCES

Beneke, T. (1982). *Men on Rape.* New York: St. Martin's.

Burgess, A., and L. Holmstrom. (1974). "Rape: Sexual Disruption and Recovery." *American Journal of Orthopsychiatry,* 49, 648.

Drukteinis, A. (1992). "Serial Murder: The Heart of Darkness. *Psychiatric Annals 22,* 532–38.

Freeman-Longo, R., and R. Wall. (1986). "Changing a Lifetime of Sexual Crime." *Psychology Today* (March): 58-64.

Greenberg, D., J. Bradford, and S. Curry. (1993). "A Comparison of Sexual Victimization in the Childhoods of Pedophiles and Hebephiles." *Journal of Forensic Sciences,* 38, 432-36.

Howell, J. (1984). Cited in D. Gelman. "Stolen Children." *Newsweek* (March 19).

Hunt, P., and M. Baird. (1990). "Children of Sex Rings." *Child Welfare 69,* 195–207.

Huttinger, B. (1984). *My Child Is Not Missing: A Parent's Guidebook for the Prevention and Recovery of Missing Children.* Plantation, FL: Child Safe Products.

Kendall-Tackett, K., L. Williams & D. Finkelhor. (1993). "Impact of Sexual Abuse on Children: A Review and Synthesis of Recent Empirical Studies. *Psychological Bulletin* 11, 164–80.

Lang, R., and R. Frenzel. (1988). "How Sex Offenders Lure Children." *Annals of Sex Research* 1, 303–17.

Lang, R., and R. Langevin. (1991). "Parent-Child Relations in Offenders who Commit Violent Sexual Crimes against Children." *Behavioral Sciences and the Law* 9, 61–71.

Lanning, K. (1994). "Child Molesters: A Behavioral Analysis." *School Safety* (Spring): 12–17.

Levant, M., and B. Bass. (1991). "Parental Identification of Rapists and Pedophiles. *Psychological Reports* 69, 463–66.

Lowenstein, L. (1992). "The Psychology of the Obsessed Compulsive Killer." *Criminologist* 16, 26-38.

Malinosky-Rummell, R., and D. Hansen. (1993). "Long-Term Consequences of Childhood Physical Abuse." *Psychological Bulletin* 114, 68-79.

Newman, S. (1985). *Never Say Yes to a Stranger.* New York: Putnam.

Peach, M., and D. Klass. (1987). "Special Issues in the Grief of Parents of Murdered Children." *Death Studies* 11, 81–88.

Quina, K., and N. Carlson. (1989). *Rape, Incest, and Sexual Harassment: A Guide for Helping Survivors.* New York: Praeger.

Russell, D. (1975). *The Politics of Rape.* New York: Stein & Day.

▌▌▌4

Noncustodial Parental Abductions

INTRODUCTION

At a recent clambake five women and five men were entrants in a game of tug of war. The five women on one side tugged and pulled the rope with all the effort they could muster; the five men did the same. This game is an apt metaphor for what happens in divorce and custody battles that may lead to a noncustodial parental abduction. The parents tug and pull the children, using them as pawns in their own struggle for custody and abuse toward the other parent. Unlike tug of war, however, children in divorce custody battles and abductions don't perceive themselves as participating in a game. In this tug of war no matter which side wins, the children always end up in the mud.

Jill Krementz (1984) compiled children's perceptions about divorce and custody in *How It Feels When Parents Divorce*. Parents are unusually so concerned with legal expenses, finding new jobs, new places of residence, that decentering from their own perspective to find out what their children feel may never occur to them, or if it does, it often does not take top priority. Nineteen children were interviewed in Krementz' book.

Meredith, fourteen, stated:

> I think that when parents do get divorced, whichever parent doesn't get custody should try to see his or her kids as much as possible. And I think that when people get divorced they shouldn't say bad things about each other to

57

kids. For example, my mother will say something like "Well, you'd better call your father this week and remind him to pick you up," as if he would forget if we didn't remind him. Those are the kind of remarks I resent. My father does it too, and I wish they would both stop. (26)

Ten-year-old Jimmy shared the following:

The court decided that I should live permanently with my Dad but keep on seeing my mother on weekends. Well, that made my mother so mad that she decided to steal me. One weekend while I was visiting her, she and Don packed up their car with a lot of stuff and we all piled in. I kept asking her, "Where are we going?" And finally she said, "Take a wild guess." I guessed a couple of places and finally I said Florida because that was the one place she had talked about a lot—she had some relatives who lived there. . . . I remember asking her, "What about Daddy?" And she just said, "Don't worry about it." (30-31)

Thirteen-year-old Gillian indicated that she shared her feelings in poetry so "no one can get mad at me and things don't stay all bottled up inside me, either" (109). One of her poems follows:

Like the Red Sea
Parted
Yet never joined again
Mommy's world
Daddy's world
So different
Sometimes I wonder
Which is better for me?
But I'll never really know. (109)

In this chapter we will discuss the impact of divorce and custody decisions on women's and men's intent to abduct their children. A consideration of the psychological impact of noncustodial parental abduction will also be presented. We will conclude this chapter with some suggestions for empowering children of divorce, including how children should be told about divorce. We'll see that Gillian's poem captured what researchers have identified for some time: there are two "worlds." There is one reality for women and another, sometimes different, for men.

TWO "WORLDS": HER MARRIAGE/HIS MARRIAGE

Jessie Bernard (1971, 1973) viewed marriage not as one institution but two—hers and his. She wrote:

> A substantial body of research shores up Emile Durkheim's conclusion that the "regulations imposed on the woman by marriage are always more stringent [than those imposed on men]. Thus she loses more and gains less from the institution." Considerable well-authenticated data show that there are actually two marriages in every marital union—his and hers—which do not always coincide. Thus, for example, when researchers ask husbands and wives identical questions about their marriages, they often get quite different replies even on fairly simple factual questions. Although in nonclinical populations roughly the same proportion of men and women say they are happy, by and large when husbands and wives are asked about specific items in their relationships, the wives' marriages look less happy than their husbands'. For as Durkheim found, marriage is not the same for women as for men. (146–47)

Why is it that marriage is believed to be different for women than for men? The answer lies, at least partially, in the unequal status and the power imbalance that marriage accords both partners. Historically, wives were thought of as little more than a husband's property (Scanzoni, 1972). We need to go back only about a hundred years to find a time when a wife was not allowed to control property, even the property she inherited from her premarriage family. According to English common law, a husband had total control over his wife. A husband controlled his wife's wages and had the last say in their children's education and religion (Chapman and Gates, 1977).

One of the more often reported studies of marriages was conducted in Detroit just over thirty-four years ago by

Robert Blood and Donald Wolfe (1960). Over nine hundred wives were questioned about who in their marriages had the final say in matters like "what job the husband should take," "what car to buy," "what doctor to call when someone in the family was sick," and "how much to spend on the weekly groceries." By and large, the study found that husbands generally made decisions about their jobs and about buying new cars, while wives decided on which doctors to call in cases of illness and how much to spend on the weekly groceries. In tabulating their results, Blood and Wolfe assumed that all decisions were relatively equal in importance; they noted that many of the families in their study appeared to have an egalitarian marriage. However, we could question the assumption that deciding to buy a new car is equivalent to deciding how much to spend on groceries. These decisions are not equivalent, and families that distribute the decision-making process along these issues are anything but egalitarian (Doyle and Paludi, 1995).

Researchers are now more apt to define two types of egalitarian marriages: syncratic and autonomic (Gray-Little and Burks, 1983). The syncratic relation describes a marital pattern in which both the wife and the husband wield power and make decisions jointly in all areas. The autonomic pattern refers to an egalitarian relationship in which husband and wife each exercise power and control over separate areas.

TWO "WORLDS": HER DIVORCE/HIS DIVORCE

Although the rate of divorce in the United States has leveled off in the last few years, it remains quite high. Currently, 4.7 divorces occur per 100,000 couples in the population, according to the U.S. Department of Health and Human Services (1990). Between 40 and 50 percent of current first marriages will end in divorce. Research also generally shows that contrary to folk wisdom, wives initiate divorce more often than husbands (Matlin, 1993). When women and men are asked about the problems in their marriage that led to separations and divorce, there are often gender differences in their responses. Kelly (1982) noted that 66 percent of the women complained that they felt unloved, in comparison with 37 percent of the men. Women also complained that their husbands belittled their competence and criticized them too much. The most common complaint from the men (53 percent) was that their wives had been inattentive, neglecting their needs and wishes. Men were also more likely than women to complain about dissimilarities in interests or values, and women were more likely to report physical violence in the marriage.

One gender similarity in the research concerns individuals' reactions to divorce. Divorce is particularly painful both for husbands and for wives because it involves so many different kinds of separation—from a spouse, from children, from friends and relatives, and loss of property previously owned. Furthermore, a newly divorced individual must learn to live independently and make decisions alone.

One common emotional reaction to divorce is anger, which women report twice as often as men (Ellwood and Stolberg, 1993). Depression is also a common reaction, equally observed among men and women. For many women, their financial situation is almost always worse following a divorce. The total family income of most divorced women and their children is less than half of their family income prior to the divorce (Arendell, 1987).

IMPACT OF DIVORCE ON CHILDREN

More than one-third of the children born in the 1970s and 1980s are expected to experience the divorce of their parents (Emery, 1988). Children who experience divorce exhibit adjustment problems that may continue for years after the divorce itself (Grych and Fincham, 1992). For example, children from divorced families exhibit higher levels of externalizing problems such as aggression and conduct disorder than children from intact families. These problems are seen both in girls and in boys, the latter exhibiting them for longer periods of time. The National Survey of Children found that boys from divorced families exhibited higher levels of antisocial behavior eight years after the divorce than boys from low-conflict, intact families (Peterson and Zill, 1986). In addition, internalizing problems such as depression, anxiety, and withdrawal also have been reported in children from divorced familes (Forehand, et al., 1990).

Grych and Fincham (1992) noted that children who experience divorce exhibit adjustment problems, particularly in the first two years following the divorce. The adjustment problems are especially apparent when one considers the time of the separation, not the final divorce decree. Many children have vivid memories of the day their mother or father left the family as opposed to the final decree, which may have occurred without their awareness. In addition, the events associated with life after divorce—such as single parenting, visitation, and economic strain—may contribute to the children's adjustment problems.

Thus, it may not be the divorce per se but subsequent events that lead to continuing adjustment problems in children (Grych and Fincham, 1992). Factors such as the consistency of parenting and the degree of conflict between ex-spouses are better predictors of children's adjustment than whether the parents have divorced. Research investigating characteristics of children that may influence their adaptation to divorce has focused on four factors: gender, age, temperament, and social cognition.

Gender

Boys exhibit higher levels of maladjustment after divorce than girls, especially when they are living with single mothers (Zaslow, 1988, 1989). When children live with a custodial father or in a remarried family, girls exhibit poorer adjustment than girls in intact homes. Boys in remarried or father-custody homes fare better than those in mother-custody homes (Peterson and Zill, 1986). These findings may be explained by the following dynamics that have been observed. First, custodial fathers and mothers differ in parenting styles. Fathers may be less likely to become involved in coercive exchanges with boys than mothers (Emery, Hetherington, and DiLalla, 1984). Custodial mothers may thus have more conflict with sons than with daughters.

Age

Judith Wallerstein (1983) reported qualitative changes in the typical reactions of children of different ages. For example, she reported that preschool children tend to regress behaviorally, blame themselves for the divorce, and fear being abandoned and separated from parents. Elementary school children commonly express moderate depression, are preoccupied with the parent's departure from the home, perceive the divorce as a rejection of them, and fear being replaced. Older children express greater anger about the divorce, tend to blame one of the parents for the divorce, and may develop somatic symptoms.

Temperament

Mavis Hetherington's (1989) research suggests that when social support is not available for children, stress has a more adverse effect on temperamentally difficult children than on temperamentally easy children.

Social Cognition

Therapists have generally stressed the importance of children gaining an accurate understanding of their parents' divorce (e.g., Wallerstin, 1983). In fact, most of the intervention programs include as a goal clarifying children's misconceptions about divorce (Pedro-Carroll and Cowen, 1987; to be discussed later in this chapter). Kurdek and Berg (1983) reported that children's attitudes about their parents' divorce include blame, hope of reunification, and fear of abandonment.

Thus, research suggests that some children's characteristics are related to their adjustment to divorce. Warshak (1992) outlined the following coping factors that can help maximize children's chances of dealing with divorce:

1. sufficient access to each parent to enable children to maintain high-quality relationships with both;

2. a cooperative, low-conflict relationship between the parents;

3. skilled and sensitive child-rearing practices;

4. minimal changes for children; and

5. good social-support systems for children and parents.

Michael Ellwood and Arnold Stolberg (1993) reported similar coping styles in their study of three groups of children aged eight to eleven: those whose parents remained married, those whose parents were divorced, and those whose parents divorced and subsequently remarried. Higher levels of family functioning were associated with families where parental hostility was low and parents displayed few rejection behaviors while practicing consistent and appropriate discipline.

Pedro Portes and his colleagues (1992) also examined the relation of various family conditions and aspects of children's adjustment. Those factors most significant in facilitating socioemotional adjustment were family roles, behavior control, and affective involvement. Families in which nurturance, mutual support, and family rituals were maintained after the divorce were more likely to minimize the maladjustment of the children. Parental conflict and animosity may have an impact on children that may be reflected in social withdrawal, anxiety, and depression.

The results of each of these studies need to be considered during child custody hearings, rather than relying on stereotypes about women, men, motherhood and fatherhood.

CHILD SUPPORT AND CUSTODY ISSUES: AVOIDING A REAL-LIFE TUG OF WAR

Inadequate or unpaid support is likely to adversely affect children's adaptation to the divorce; it creates economic hardship for custodial parents and children. Furthermore, children whose noncustodial parents are not making support payments are frequently caught in interparental conflict.

Increased interest in divorce intervention programs has been prompted by the desire to preserve relationships the child has with both parents in the hope of ensuring children's well-being following divorce. The type of custody arrangement influences children's adjustment after the divorce. Maccoby, Depner and Mnookin (1990) reported greater cooperation between parents who were sharing custody of their children.

There is some confusion over the meaning of shared custody or joint custody. Joint legal custody means that parents divide authority so that each retains the right to make decisions in some sphere. For example, one parent may retain the sole right to select her children's place of worship while she is willing to share decisions regarding medical care and education. Joint legal custody also means that both parents are legally responsible for the actions of their minor children. This arrangment may or may not include joint physical custody. Joint physical custody, also referred to as "joint residential custody" means that the children's time in each parent's household is more evenly balanced than occurs in sole custody and approximates a fifty-fifty split.

Research has suggested that rather than being used to express their parents' hostility, children in joint custody witness less tension and more cooperation between their parents than do children in traditional sole-custody arrangements (Pearson and Thoennes, 1990). Joint custody in itself probably does not reduce the strain between ex-spouses; the parents were probably more cooperative to begin with. Their ability to maintain a collaborative relationship for their children eases the strain of divorce for their children. Parents who have joint custody are more likely than parents with sole custody to conform with the following guidelines Pearson and Thoennes (1990) identified in their study as helping children of divorce avoid psychological problems:

1. Cooperate with each other.

2. Avoid physical violence in the home.

3. Maintain children's regular access to each parent.

4. Minimize the number of changes in the children's lives (e.g., moving, changing schools).

Joint custody arrangements are apt to inhibit one parent kidnapping her or his child from the ex-spouse.

NONCUSTODIAL PARENTAL ABDUCTION: A REAL-LIFE TUG OF WAR

One response to the outcome of divorce is one parent kidnapping or abducting his or her child from the other parent, the latter of whom has been awarded sole custody of the child. It has been estimated that between 300 and 600 thousand children are abducted by their parents each year. Finkelhor and Dzuiba-Leatherman (1994) recently reported that 81 percent of child victimizations involve a parental abduction. A child is most vulnerable to this form of victimization before either parent has been awarded custody.

The prime targets for parental abductions are children between three and eleven, with those between three and five the most likely victims. Children younger than three are typically not abducted by a noncustodial parent because they create unique problems for the abductor: they need constant supervision and care. Children older than eleven are likely to telephone home, run away, or alert law-enforcement agencies (Hyde and Hyde, 1985).

Rebecca Hegar and Geoffrey Greif (1991) surveyed 371 parents who requested assistance from missing children's organizations in order to provide a profile of families in which children were abducted by one of the parents. Abductors were characterized as less educated and less likely to be employed than searching parents. In addition, three-fourths of abducted children were six or younger. The majority of abductions involved a single child, and the abducting parents tended to be male (55 percent). Mothers whose children were kidnapped by their fathers described more violence in their marriages, more fault-related reasons for divorce, and more force used in the abduction than did fathers whose children were kidnapped by their mothers.

Cole and Bradford (1992) found similar results in their study of twenty cases of child abductions during divorce custody and access disputes. These twenty cases involved twenty parents and thirty-seven children; they were examined after the children had been returned to the custodial parent. Cole and Bradford compared the characteristics of the abduction to those of a control population of twenty custodial disputes not involving abduction. Compared to control parents, abducting parents were more likely to be male, born outside of America, with previous psychiatric contact, and with previous criminal charges.

Children abducted by noncustodial parents are typically told that the other parent is unfit, dead, or will kill them if they return. They are also frequently told that the other parent has a new family and is not interested in having them returned. The psychological impact of being abducted by a parent and living with this individual is stressful for children. Children experience fear, grief over the loss of the other parent, confusion about divorce and their role in it, guilt for not calling the other parent, and hatred for the parents (Abrahms, 1983). As is true with children and adolescents who are runaways or abducted by strangers, those children who are abducted by a parent suffer long-term emotional and physical stress-related symptoms. They view themselves as pawns between their feuding parents; consequently they have little opportunity to develop a sense of trust, an important part in the development of an identity. Many of these children are also physically and sexually abused by their abducting parents. Children thus learn to view the world in general as a hostile place where people can't be trusted and where they are only seen as worthy if they are useful to someone else.

Sally Abrahms in *Children in the Crossfire*, reported that malice is the most common motive for parental abductors. United Parents against Child Stealing, an organzation in Arizona that assists abduction victims, has estimated that eight out of ten parents abduct their children strictly for revenge. Abrahms recounted the following illustration of this "get-even mentality": "Thirteen-year-old Judy of Detroit, stolen twice, remembers hearing her father threaten her mother: 'I'll get back at you. I'll get you,' he used to tell her.' " (126). As

Abrahms concludes, "In this pitiful war between the parents, it is the kids who are caught in the crossfire" (xix).

The American Bar Association estimates that parents who lose their children through parental abduction have only three chances in ten of finding them. Parental abductors move frequently; their income tax returns or Social Security records are not of much use. The Parental Kidnapping Prevention Act of 1980 was the initial federal statute passed to make parental abduction a federal crime. In 1932 the Lindberg Act was signed into federal law; this excluded kidnapping by parents, however. On December 28, 1980, a portion of the Fugitive Felon Act took effect. This is designed to provide FBI assistance to state and local law enforcement personnel in investigating state felony child abduction and restrain cases that involve interstate flight. This law creates a "legal maze" (Hyde and Hyde, 1985) for custodial parents since there is no uniform method to parental kidnapping at the state level.

At the state level, the statutes dealing with child abductions by noncustodial parents are referred to by a variety of names, including "custodial interference," "child restraint," and "parental kidnapping." Some states have felony child abduction and restraint statutes; others have misdemeanor statutes, still others have felony statutes. Law enforcement officials are occasionally reluctant to get involved in custody situations. Relying on the strength of a warrant for extradition charges can be futile, particularly if there is no cooperation between states. Adding to the frustration is the apparent leniency shown the abductor. The penalty for committing the act of abduction is typically weak. Consequently, the penalty does not deter an individual from committing the crime or repeating it thereafter.

Most custodial parents get assistance from family, friends, and the community in trying to find their abducted children. The search is very difficult and in most cases is futile. Geoffrey Grief and Rebecca Hegar (1993) suggest that noncustodial parental abduction is on the increase and may rise even further as a result of the relaxation of travel barriers between countries. To deal with her own grief over her daughter's abduction by the daughter's father, Gloria Yerkovich founded Child Find, Incorporated, a national organization devoted to reuniting missing children and their custodial parents. Among its services is a toll-free hotline, available for any child searching for a parent as well as any adult who can assist in identifying a missing child. Support groups for custodial parents have proven to be helpful, since the parent and other family members and friends respond to the abduction with lasting emotional and physical stress-related symptoms.

SUMMARY

The research cited in this chapter is quite clear: efforts to change laws and legal policies pertaining to divorce are needed to facilitate children's adaptation to divorce by reducing environmental stress and economic hardship after divorce. In addition to legislation (see chapter 7), intervention programs must be utilized in order to help children cope with divorce and the new lifestyle it brings with it. One type of intervention is a child-centered approach that attempts to help children by alleviating the negative feelings, practical problems, and misconceptions that typically are experienced following a divorce. These programs use a small-group format of four to ten children. Discussions about divorce with peers who also are dealing with divorce and its aftermath normalize the experience and provide a supportive network for children (Pedro-Carroll and Cowen, 1987). Sessions include a variety of techniques, including role playing, use of audiovisual materials, storytelling, social problem-solving exercises, drawing, and creating plays or newspapers that deal with divorce. According to Grych and Fincham (1992), such child-centered groups are common. One program designed by Kalter and colleagues (1988) has been used in more than two thousand school districts and one hundred mental health facilites since its inception.

Joanne Pedro-Carroll and her colleagues (1985) have developed the Children of Divorce Intervention Project. In addition to the issues Kalter's program deals with, the CODIP program seeks to enhance children's perceptions of themselves and their families. Follow-up research with this intervention project indicates that according to teacher ratings, children participaing in this project showed a greater decrease in shyness and anxiety problems and a greater increase in adaptive assertiveness and frustration tolerance than the comparison groups. Pedro-Carroll and Cowen (1985) also noted that children exhibited a greater decrease in learning problems and increases in peer sociability and rule compliance.

Both of these intervention programs recognize the fact that while it may be difficult to reduce stress in the lives of children of divorce, it is possible to affect children's adjustment by altering their perception of and response to stressful circumstances. Thus, intervention programs that are family focused are helpful in this regard. Such intervention programs deal with parenting and parent-child relationships, coping with changes that marital dissolution brings and unique problems faced by custodial parents (e.g., Wolchik, et al., 1988). These programs also aim to increase the amount of contact the child has with the noncustodial parent and with nonparental adults. Thus, these programs promote children's well-being by enabling parents to be more effective in their roles.

Learning parenting skills can help individuals recognize what Margaret Strickland, whose grandson was abducted, once stated: "To steal a child is not an act of love; it is an act of selfishness." Or, as Jimmy, a child abducted first by his mother and then by his father, and whose opinion was given voice at the beginning of this chapter quipped:

> When I think back over the past eight years, it seems as if I was just in one court and out the other, and half the time I didn't know what was going on. I went to about four different psychiatrists, but they didn't help, and the kids at school teased me when they found out I was going. Also, the doctors would always promise not to tell my father and new mother what I said, but a couple of them did tell, anyway, who wants to talk to a total stranger about his problems? I don't. I just want to get on with my life and forget what happened. . . . I'm keeping my fingers crossed that everything will work out. (33–35)

It is only through listening to children like Jimmy that we can undestand how parental abductions leave their mark on children's lives.

REFERENCES

Abrahms, S. (1983). *Children in the Crossfire: The Tragedy of Parental Kidnapping.* New York: Atheneum.

Arendell, T. (1987). "Women and the Economics of Divorce in the Contemporary United States." *Signs* 13, 121–35.

Bernard, J. (1971). "The Paradox of the Happy Marriage." In V. Gornick and B. Moran (eds.), *Women in Sexist Society.* New York: American Library.

Blood, R., and D. Wolfe. (1960). *Husbands and Wives.* New York: Free Press.

Chapman, J., and M. Gates. (eds.) (1977). *Forcible Rape.* New York: Columbia University Press.

Cole, W., and J. Bradford. (1992). "Abduction during Custody and Access Disputes." *Canadian Journal of Psychiatry* 37, 264–66.

Doyle, J., and M. Paludi. (1995). *Sex and Gender.* Dubuque: Wm. C. Brown.

Ellwood, M., and A. Stolberg. (1993). "The Effects of Family Composition, Family Health, Parenting Behavior and Environmental Stress on Children's Divorce Adjustment. *Journal of Child and Family Studies* 2, 23-36.

Emery, R. (1988). *Marriage, Divorce, and Children's Adjustment.* Newbury Park, CA: Sage.

Emery, R., E. M. Hetherington, and L. DiLalla. (1984). "Divorce, Children, and Social Policy." In H. Stevenson and A. Siegel (eds.), *Child Development Research and Social Policy.* Chicago: University of Chicago Press.

Finkelhor, D., and J. Dziuba-Leatherman. (1994). "Victimization of Children." *American Psychologist* 49, 173–83.

Forehand, R., A. Thomas, M. Wierson, G. Brody, and R. Fauber. (1990). "Role of Maternal Functioning and Parenting Skills in Adolescent Functioning Following Parental Divorce. *Journal of Abnormal Psychology* 99, 278–83.

Gray-Little, B., and N. Burks. (1983). "Power and Satisfaction in Marriage: A Review and Critique. *Psychological Bulletin* 93, 513–38.

Grief, G., and R. Hegar. (1993). "International Parental Abduction and Its Implications for Social Work Practice: Great Britain to the United States." *Children and Society* 7, 269–76.

Grych, J., and F. Fincham. (1992). "Interventions for Children of Divorce: Toward Greater Integration of Research and Action. *Psychological Bulletin* 111, 434–54.

Heger, R., and F. Grief. (1991). "Abduction of Children by Their Parents: A Survey of the Problem." *Social Work* 36, 421–26.

Hetherington, E. M. (1989). "Coping with Family Transitions: Winners, Losers, and Survivors. *Child Development* 60, 1-14.

Hyde, M., and L. Hyde. (1985). *Missing Children*. New York: Franklin Watts.

Kalter, N., D. Alpern, J. Falk, M. Gittleman, M. Markow, K. Okla, J. Pickar, S. Rubin, M. Schaefer, and S. Schreier. (1988). *Children of Divorce: Facilitation of Development through School-Based Groups* [manual]. Lansing: Michigan Department of Health.

Kelly, J. B. (1982). "Divorce: The Adult Perspective." In B. B. Wolman (ed.), *Handbook of Developmental Psychology*. Englewood Cliffs, NJ: Prentice Hall.

Krementz, J. (1984). *How It Feels When Parents Divorce*. New York: Knopf.

Kurdek, L., and B. Berg. (1983). "Correlates of Children's Adjustment to Their Parents' Divorces." In L. Krudek (ed.), *New Directions in Child Development*. San Francisco: Jossey Bass.

Maccoby, E. E., C. Depner, and R. Mnookin. (1990). "Co-parenting in the Second Year After Divorce." *Journal of Marriage and the Family* 52, 141–55.

Matlin, M. (1993). *The Psychology of Women*. New York: Harcourt Brace Jovanovich.

Pedro-Carroll, J., and E. Cowen. (1985). "The Children of Divorce Intervention Program: An Investigtion of the Efficacy of School-Based Prevention Program. *Journal of Consulting and Clinical Psychology* 53, 603–11.

Pearson, J., and N. Thoennes. (1990). Custody after divorce: Demographic and attitudinal patterns. *American Journal of Orthopsychiatry* 60, 233–49.

Petersen, J., and N. Zill. (1986). "Marital Disruption, Parent-Child Relationships and Behavior Problems in Children." *Journal of Marriage and the Family* 48, 295–307.

Portes, P., S. Howell, J. Brown, and S. Eichenberger. (1992). "Family Functions and Children's Postdivorce Adjustment." *American Journal of Orthopsychiatry* 62, 613–17.

Scanzoni, J. (1972). *Sexual Bargaining.* Englewood Cliffs, NJ: Prentice Hall.

Strickland, M. (1983). *How to Deal with a Parental Kidnapping.* Moorehaven, FL: Rainbow.

United States Department of Health and Human Servies (1990). *Monthly Vital Statistics Report* 13, No. 13.

Wallerstein, J. (1983). "Children of Divorce: Stress and Developmental Tasks." In N. Garmezy and M. Rutter (eds.), *Stress, Coping and Development in Children.* New York: McGraw Hill.

Warshak, R. (1992). *The Custody Revolution.* New York: Poseidon Press.

Wolchik, S., S. Westover, G. West, I. Sandler, and P. Balls. (1988). "Translating Empirical Findings into an Intervention for Children of Divorce." Paper presented at the ninety-sixth Annual Convention of the American Psychological Association, Atlanta, GA.

Zaslow, M. (1988). "Sex Differences in Children's Response to Parental Divorce: Research Methodology and Postdivorce Family Form." *American Journal of Orthopsychiatry* 58, 355–78.

———. (1989). "Sex Differences in Children's Response to Parental Divorce: Samples, Variables, Ages, and Sources." *American Journal of Orthopsychiatry* 59, 118–41.

Part Three

Responsibility of Parents, Schools, and Legislators in Dealing with Missing Children

▌▌▌5

The Role and Responsibilities of Parents

INTRODUCTION

Have you ever browsed through a bookstore in the section on parenting and parent-child relations? You will see books after books after books on how to parent. You'll find titles such as the following:

Mother Care/Other Care
Toddlers and Parents
Positive Parenting
The Challenge of Parenthood
Today's Children
Family Rules
Teaching Your Children Responsibility
What Do You Really Want for Your Children?
Parent Power

You will find books that offer suggestions on what to feed infants and toddlers, how to toilet train them, how to select quality day care, disciplining techniques, the role of play in child development, and sibling rivalry. You may even locate some books dealing with "special" parenting issues, such as, single parenting, lesbian parenting, gay parenting, divorce, adoptive parenting, stepparenting, communal parenting, and parenting physically challenged children. The fact that there are so many books published on parenting each year suggests that people feel ill equiped to raise children. They may not want to model their own parenting style after the way they were raised. Or perhaps they want to read about what "parenting experts" have to say on how to raise a happy and healthy child. Or some people may not live near or with extended family members (our support networks) who could act as "mentors." Whatever the reason, most people still feel unprepared to take on the enormous responsibility of child rearing. Very few people take courses in parenting and, if they do, most classes are theoretical, not based in practical experiences. Parents thus seek information so we do the best job we can in bringing up the next generation.

During our recent review of hundreds of books for parents, we were amazed at the lack of information provided on keeping children safe. We looked through countless numbers of indices for mention of: stranger abductions, missing children, child abuse, runaways, and child safety rules. None of these subjects was listed. In one book, *Parents on the Spot,* however, author Judi Craig (1994) offered a page of suggestions to parents to help their children not get in conversations with strangers. In another book, *Positive Parenting from A to Z,* Joslin (1994) suggested parents tell their children "not to talk to strangers." For the most part, that was the extent of advice for parents in dealing with the very essence of what this book is about.

Why does so little information exist about child abductions and missing children in popular books for parents? We discounted the explanation that there is insufficient information on the topics of child abductions and abuse, and also discounted the explanation that authors believe the topic of missing children is not an important topic to cover in books for parents. Perhaps authors believe that parents want to know about those issues all babies experience—language development, growth trends, bedtime problems, for example—and not about rarer experiences. One look at the statistics on childhood victimizations would counter this belief, however.

Child development and parenting experts tend to focus their efforts on issues related to children becoming indepen-

dent from parents, becoming autonomous, respecting authority, behaving according to social rules, and living by the "golden
rule," teaching that if we treat others nicely, they will do the
same for us. Unfortunately, the "expert" advice presented in
some parenting books runs counter to the way we should be
raising "street smart" children.

   This chapter offers several suggestions for ways parents
can teach themselves and their children about child abductions
and missing children. Included are some suggested reading
materials and organizations from which parents can obtain
additional information on how to talk with their children about
victimzation. As Penelope Leach (1994) wrote in her latest
book, *Children First: What Our Society Must Do and Is Not
Doing for Our Children Today*:

> Children are a large part of many people's present and the
> whole of everybody's future. The richest societies, the most
> democratic governments and the most complex social in-
> stitutions the world has ever known . . . fail to meet many
> children's acknowledged needs. It cannot be good enough
> because they can do better. (26)

It is because we share Leach's sentiment about educating children through educating parents that we present the following
suggestions for lessons for life.

FROM RESEARCH AND THEORY TO PRACTICAL ADVICE

Knowledge of several characteristics of abductors—both strangers and parental—which have already been mentioned will be
helpful for parents in educating their children about becoming
street smart. We will briefly list these characteristics again:

1. Most abductors select their victims carefully before at-
   tacking.

2. Abductors try to lure children into coming with them
   rather than resort to physical violence.

3. No child abductor wants to be caught.

4. Abductors seek information from children so as to later use it as a way to keep children from leaving.

5. Abductors prey on children's fears or emotions to lure them into a car.

6. Abductors use authoritative means to intimidate children into accompanying them.

There are several steps parents can take to make their children less vulnerable to abductors.

1. Parents must teach their children their full name, address (including state), and telephone number (including area code). Children who do not know their complete name, address, and/or phone number are likely to panic and be unable to call for help or get home.

2. Parents must teach children how to dial either 911 or 0 (for the operator). Children must be encouraged to practice dialing these numbers and be provided information (in language they can understand) about the importance of knowing how to do this task.

3. Parents and children should select a "codeword" or "codephrase" with which the child is familiar (e.g., a favorite food, TV show). Parents should tell children that if they are approached by someone who uses the codeword, that this means it is safe to accompany this individual. Once the codeword is used, it is advisable to change it to prevent it from being inadvertently disclosed to other individuals. Children must be taught never to tell anyone the codeword.

4. Parents should not purchase any articles of clothing or school supplies with their children's names on them. Children will respond more readily to a stranger if they are addressed by name. This is how abductors begin to establish a rapport with children. Should children want monogramed items, parents can purchase a toothbrush, comb, drinking cup or any other item that will remain in the home.

5. Parents should teach their children the names for parts of their bodies. Many children do not know the names for their genitals. Should parents or children feel awkward in using the correct language, children can instead be taught to say "the part of my body that's private" or "the part of my body that's covered by underwear."

6. When children know the parts of their bodies, parents can then teach them the difference between "good touch" and "bad touch." A useful guide in this regard is the following. Parents should tell their children that a "good touch" makes you feel right, wanted, cared for. A "bad touch" is unwanted and does not feel good.

7. Children should not be taught by parents to give unconditional affection. If children don't want to kiss or hug an aunt or uncle, their wishes should be respected. By telling unwilling children to give a hug or kiss to someone, parents are giving them the message that forced physical contact is acceptable. This message is a dangerous one to send, for children may rely on the message with an abductor, and believe the touching and other unwanted behavior is allowed.

8. Parents need to identify uniformed individuals to whom their children can go for help should they become separated from the parents. For example, should a child get separated from her parents in a store at a mall, the child should know to go to the nearest checkout counter and ask a clerk for assistance.

9. Children need to be taught to never answer the door or phone when they are home alone or to tell anyone that they are alone in the house.

10. Parents must tell babysitters never to release children under any circumstances to anyone except someone designated by the parents themselves.

HOW PARENTS MUST TEACH CHILDREN
ABOUT ABDUCTIONS AND VICTIMIZATION

Research and experience have suggested that simply utilizing the information listed above will not ensure that chidren will act "street smart" if confronted by an abductor. Cheryl Poche (1988) assigned seventy-four kindergarten and first-grade children to a variety of conditions designed to evaluate methods of teaching self-protection. She reported that a videotape training program accompanied by behavior rehearsal proved highly effective in teaching safe responses to potential abductors. Three-fourths of the children who received no training immediately agreed to accompany "suspects."

Behavioral rehearsal can take the form of a game for younger children. This game has been referred to by some as the "what if" game. For example, parents can tell their children they are going to pretend. Then parents ask a question, for example, "What if you and Mommy went to the grocery store to buy food for KittyCat. And, you and Mommy got separated. What would you do?" As another example a parent might say, "Let's pretend what you would do if you were walking home from school and someone you did not know stopped to talk." It is important for parents to provide alternatives to this story for their children and ask for responses. Parents need to ask for lengthy answers to be sure the children understand the issues.

Paula Geonie, founder and president of Playing It Safe, a safety program for children that includes a component on strangers (see figure 5.1), also recommends the use of flashcards and songs for children to reinforce the messages concerning fleeing a potential abductor. She has also devised "puppet pals" for use in behavioral rehearsal in a variety of situations, for example, "A stranger pulls her car over and asks you for directions. What should you do?" Children are asked to use the puppets in acting out their responses to the scenario.

In *Let's Be Safe,* Dailing (1994) offers a poem that can be used in educating children about what to do when confronted with a stranger. The following is an excerpt from the poem:

Big people should not ask little people for help.

Figure 5.1   Big people should not ask little people for help. If anyone asks you for help, even if it is someone you know, you must get permission from the person taking care of you. If someone asks you for directions or wants you to help find a pet, what should you do? From P. Geonie, Playing It Safe: A Child's Guide to Personal Safety." Reprinted with permission from Paula Geonie.

So that is why you must not talk to strangers that you meet;

don't let them give you any toys, or anything to eat.

If someone that you do not know should offer you a treat,

remember how he [sic] looks and talks, but run fast up the street. (27)

It is recommended that parents, when using behavioral rehearsal or other teaching tools, define the term *stranger* for their children. In a 1987 program on HBO entitled "How to

Raise a Street Smart Child," several young children were asked who they thought a stranger was. Responses included:

A bad guy.

Wears glasses.

Puts a coat over his mouth.

Is an alien.

Wears a brown coat.

Is a punk rocker.

Has a beard or a mustache.

Is bigger than most people.

These responses illustrate the fact that children don't know who strangers are and may think that people who could be potential abductors—if they don't meet the child's own definition of stranger—would not harm them. Parents must help their children understand that a stranger is someone you and they don't know very well. Parents may want to distinguish between "good" strangers and "bad" strangers and tell their children that "good" strangers let a child alone. Parents also need to decenter from their own perspective and understand that their children's definition of a stranger is different from their own. Children may believe a stranger is someone they've never seen before. Thus, parents must broaden their definition of a stranger and tell their children that it means any person they have not been introduced to by someone they know. It is also important for parents to help their children understand that a friend is not someone they only know by sight; that a friend is someone who is a guest in your home, not someone who comes to the door.

Parents must teach their children—through behavioral rehearsal—that it is permissible to say "No," to run away from a potential abductor, and to tell someone about their experiences. This deals with empowering children to feel that no one has the right to touch them, or make them feel uncomfortable, or ask them to keep a secret from their parents.

Another element of empowering children in this regard is for parents to teach them that if any incident occurs it is not the child's fault.

Thus, the techniques used by parents to teach their children about safety from abductions are nonthreatening for the children and designed to be empowering for them. They are designed to encourage children to trust their feelings and take action, to run, yell, and tell about their experiences. These techniques are created to put control back into the lives of children.

EXAMPLES OF BEHAVIORAL REHEARSAL WITH CHILDREN

Mother: Let's pretend you and Mommy went to the grocery store to buy food for KittyCat. The grocery store is very big isn't it?

Child: Yes. The store has lots of food to eat.

Mother: Yes. It does. And, many many people go there to buy food. Right?

Child: Hm Hm.

Mother: What if you and Mommy got separated in the big store with lots of people.
What would you do?

Child: I would feel sad and cry.

Mother: I know you would feel afraid. It can be scary to be alone away from Mommy in the big store. Mommy will always try to keep you close to her in the grocery store and everyplace else we go. Mommy loves you very much and will keep you safe.

Child: Hm Hm.

Mother: Mommy needs to know what you would do if you and Mommy ever got separated at the grocery store. What would you do?

Child: I would yell out: Where's my mommy? I can't find my mommy.

Mother: You would want someone to help you find Mommy. Wouldn't you?

Child: Yes.

Mother: I am happy that you would ask for help. Honey, Mommy doesn't want you to yell out loud in the store so everybody could hear. Some people may not help you find Mommy. But you know the best thing to do?

Child: What Mommy?

Mother: Go behind the counter and tell a man or a woman who wears the store uniform that you need to find your Mommy.

Child: Who?

Mother: Honey, remember when we buy the food for KittyCat and our food and we stand in line? Then we have a man or a woman tell us how much money we have to pay the store for the food? And, then someone puts everything we bought into bags so we can take them home?

Child: Yes, Mommy.

Mother: And, remember when we bought some chicken for dinner and we talked to that man behind the counter who wrapped the chicken for us?

Child: Hm hm.

Mother: These are the people you can talk to if you and Mommy ever got separated. You can tell the lady or man who wear a uniform. That's all. You can't tell anyone else. You can't yell in the store so everybody can hear. Now, let's go to the store and see these people. We'll play pretend some more while we are at the store. . . .

WHAT PARENTS MUST DO TO TEACH THEMSELVES ABOUT MISSING CHILDREN AND ABDUCTIONS

Parents must also become street smart themselves and take the following recommended responsibilities:

1.   Know their children's friends.

2. Make a mental note of what their children are wearing every day.

3. Ensure that their children's day care or school will phone them if their children are absent and the parents have not called and not released their children to anyone but the parents or designee.

4. Never leave their children alone or unattended in the car.

5. Make arrangements for and with their children in case of emergency.

6. Never let their children go into a public restroom alone.

7. Be involved in their children's activities.

8. Find out why an individual is showing their children a great deal of attention.

9. Be sensitive to changes in children's behavior and attitudes. Children communicate in a variety of ways. Parents must question why children don't want to be with someone.

10. Never belittle any fear children express to them.

11. Set up an atmosphere of warmth and love so that children will come to them for help if something is troubling them.

PARENTS' RIGHTS

If a child is missing, parents have several rights, including:

1. Going to the police.

2. Getting their child's name listed as a missing person with the FBI.

3. Contacting media for assistance in locating the child.

4. Getting a warrant for arrest of the noncustodial parent, if there is a suspicion of kidnapping.

To assist the police and media with locating their child, parents should obtain and keep on file the following:

1. A full description of their child, including height, weight, coloring, and any distinguishing marks.

2. A recent photograph of their child. Parents should have photographs taken at regular intervals throughout the year. If the child is under two, then at least four photographs must be taken per year.

3. Dental records.

4. Medical history.

5. Fingerprints.

THERAPEUTIC SUPPORT FOR PARENTS AND OTHER FAMILY MEMBERS

In addition to these parental rights, parents whose children are missing should seek therapeutic support, especially during the initial acute crisis phase, which generally lasts up to six weeks, depending on the severity of the experience and the support received.

Parents and other family members will experience psychological trauma as a response to the sudden and unexpected abduction in which they believe their child's life is in danger. In the immediate aftermath of a traumatic victimization experience, family members will have a number of emotional reactions—such as, helplessness, rage, terror. The stress of this trauma can also cause physical complaints, such as gastrointestinal distress, nausea, shaking, and sleep disturbances (Quina and Carlson, 1989).

Support Groups

Support groups for families of missing children can be helpful. Support groups typically break through the isolated individualism created by the abduction or kidnapping and enable family members to see their problems as social, not personal.

Facilitators of support groups for families of missing children help individuals cope with their feelings of anger and frustration and also provide strategies for handling an investigation of the abduction. Sample topics for support groups for families of missing children include:

1. accepting reality of abduction and abuse,

2. myths and facts regarding abduction,

3. guilt and responsibility,

4. nightmares,

5. family dynamics,

6. anger,

7. power,

8. physical manifestations,

9. fears

10. isolation and withdrawal from family members,

11. self-destructive coping behaviors (e.g., eating disorders, substance abuse), and

12. skills (e.g., decision making, relaxation training, parenting skills).

These topics for discussion can prove to be very helpful since a child's abduction or kidnapping affects family members' life areas, from social to sense of self (Courtois, 1988). For example:

Social: Family members feel isolated, different from others whose children are still with their families, unable to interact, mistrustful of people.

Emotional: Family members report feeling a lack of control in their lives; powerlessness.

Sexual: Family members suffer from confusion and fears of intimacy because of fear of being blamed for their child's abduction. They also feel hostility.

Familial: Family members feel estranged from other children in family and from the spouse who was with the child prior to the abduction.

Sense of Self: Family members also feel shame and powerlessness.

The goals of a support group for families of missing children are to:

1. listen to and respect individuals' reactions to being victims of a child's abduction;

2. sort out sound choices with respect to dealing with the victimization;

3. become aware of the commonality of themes in group members' lives;

4. discuss psychological issues involved in dealing with child abductions and missing children;

5. discuss the physical and emotional reactions to being a loved one of a missing child;

6. provide a psychological profile of abductors and kidnappers;

7. discuss means of resolution for finding children.

Responsibilities of support-group members include

1. agreeing to avoid judging and to focus on support and positive statements to each person, even when making a difficult comment;

2. agreeing upon and honoring time arrangements (both beginning and end);

3. clear, gentle, and nurturing confronting;

4. agreeing to come to every meeting unless it is impossible to do so;

5. keeping confidential information confidential;

6. respecting privacy at all times;

7. maintaining an atmosphere of safety and security at all times;

8. taking the responsibility of self-care.

Individual Counseling

In addition to or in lieu of a support group, family members may opt for individual resolution counseling. Paula Lundberg-Love (1987) developed an eight-step model for adult survivors of incest that may be used for family members as well. These steps are:

1. Establish rapport

    a. Enhance trust

    b. Relaxation techniques

2. Negotiate the relationship

3. Take general history

4. Take specific abuse/abduction history

    a. Memory retrieval

    b. Details of abduction

    c. Specific issues raised by abduction

5. Come to catharsis and resolution of emotional reactions

6. Reconstruct self-concept and self-esteem

7. Practice behavioral skills and stragegies for change

8. Develop future goals and plans.

The goals of this type of counseling are to help family members reformulate beliefs about the abduction and abuse— to experience "cognitive readjustment." Successful cognitive readjustment of beliefs includes a discovered abilty to cope, learn, adapt, and become self-reliant. Cognitive readjustment produces a greater sense of self-confidence, maturity, honesty, and strength. The cognitive readjustment process involves three themes: (1) the search for meaning—"Why did this happen to my child and our family?"; (2) attempts to gain mastery and control in one's life—"How can I prevent further victimization to my family?"; and (3) attempts to promote self-enhancement—"Now that my family and I have experienced this victimization, who are we?"

Spiritual Counseling

It is recommended that spiritual counseling be available for family members who request this guidance. A common religious issue to be dealt with concerns loss of an earlier faith that being "good" would protect the individual from any victimization. This loss of faith can be frightening to parents and typically involves forms of grief. Individuals should be permitted to express these doubts in a nonjudgmental atmosphere and be assured that it is normal for people to raise these questions. Pastoral counseling can be helpful in working with family members toward adopting a belief system in which concepts of "good" and "bad" are replaced by a view of the world in which other people's actions cannot be controlled.

SUMMARY

We began this chapter with an overview of the lack of popularly written material available for parents concerning child abductions and missing children. In all of the books we reviewed, there were references to a developmentally normative event referred to as "fear of strangers." At approximately five and eight months of age, an infant's memory develops so that the baby can remember familiar people and be wary of individuals who are not familiar to them. Most infants at this age resist attention from individuals—including extended family members they do not see often—they don't know well. Child development experts try to reassure parents that this stranger anxiety or fear of strangers will decline after fifteen months and is quite rare by the time the child is three. One text used the following illustration: "Jason may not want to stay with his babysitter . . . he feels 'stranger axiety' toward the unfamiliar teenager. His reaction is normal and not an omen of a lifetime of dependence" (Papalia and Olds, 1990, 272). The wrong messages are being conveyed to parents. Is being wary of strangers a sign of dependence and therefore abnormal development while seeking out a distressing situation is a sign of autonomy and health?

Parents teaching children about becoming street smart or street wise is the best form of prevention. Law-enforcement officials are confident that the measures parents can take to teach their children how to avoid a potential abduction do make a difference. Parents need to make children comfortable about reporting situations when someone has approached them or touched them inappropriately. Children's ability to disclose such information will assist law enforcement personnel in investigations. Parents must talk with children about these lessons in life.

In the next chapter we continue our recommendations for educating children by discussing the role teachers and school administrators must play in securing a safe childhood for our youngsters.

REFERENCES

Courtois, C. (1988). *Healing the Incest Wound: Adult Survivors in Therapy.* New York: Norton.

Craig, J. (1994). *Parents on the Spot.* New York: Skylight Press.

Dailing, R. (1994). *Let's Be Safe.* New York: Chronicle Press.

Joslin, A. (1994). *Positive Parenting from A to Z.* New York: Fawcett.

Leach, P. (1994). *Children First.* New York: Knopf.

Lundberg-Love, P. (1987). *Treatment for Incest Survivors.* Paper presented at the Midwestern Society for Feminist Studies, Akron, OH.

Papalia, D., and S. W. Olds, (1990). *A Child's World: Infancy through Adolescence.* New York: McGraw-Hill.

Poche, C. (1988). "Teaching Self-Protection to Children Using Television Techniques." *Journal of Applied Behavioral Analysis* 21, 253–61.

Quina, K., and N. Carlson. (1989). *Rape, Incest, and Sexual Harassment: A Guide for Helping Survivors.* New York: Praeger.

‖‖6

The Role and
Responsibilities of Schools

INTRODUCTION

This chapter was begun a few days after a major victory was won for children in New York State: A bill was approved and signed into law by the state legislature that will make it possible for all schoolchildren in the state, through eighth grade, to receive instruction on how to protect themselves from abduction. This bill, which was sponsored by James Tedisco, will direct the commissioner of education to provide technical assistance in the development of curricula appropriate to each grade, kindergarten through eighth, and allows local boards of education to establish local advisory councils (parents, board members, law-enforcement officials, etc.) to advise the board about the development of these educational programs. One million dollars was allocated in the New York state budget for 1994 through 1995 to assist school districts in establishing the curricula.

The passage of this bill demonstrates a commitment by New York State legislators to protect children. It also recognizes the valuable role teachers and other children can play in "mentoring" children about important steps to avoid potential abductions. The curricula that will be developed will promote and maintain positive student attitudes and behavior and assist students in meeting their responsibilities to help insure the saftey and welfare of themselves and others. Similar commitments have been expressed by other state legislatures, an issue to which we will return in chapter 7.

In this chapter we offer some suggestions for curricula, teachers, and students themselves in an effort to encourage responsible conduct. Surveys of individuals' (including children's) attitudes toward child abductions and missing children suggest that the nature of this form of victimization is widely misunderstood. Educating individuals about child abductions must therefore begin with explanations of the nature of the problem before any remedy is possible.

Curriculum training programs that make us disclose what is still a hidden issue create an empowering learning and working atmosphere for all individuals. Effective training in child abductions and missing children is an important concern to all who care about children.

GOALS OF CURRICULUM PROJECTS

The specific goals of curriculum projects are the following:

1. Educate all school children about the legal definitions and behavioral examples of abductions, including situations that could cause conflict.

2. Define "missing," including nonparental abductions, runaways, and stranger abductions.

3. Discuss the physical and emotional reactions to being victimized by an abductor.

4. Provide children and adolescents with a clear understanding of their rights and responsibilities.

5. Encourage children and adolescents to examine their personal feelings and those of others.

6. Define "stranger" to include family friend, neighbor, and distant relative.

7. Explore responsible behavior in dealing with potential abductors.

8. Introduce the concept of "unsafe" places.

9. Examine the effects of an abduction on individuals, their families, and friends.

10. Distinguish between positive and negative solutions to conflict.

11. Empower children and adolescents to take control of their bodies.

Thus, curriculum training programs involve much more than a recitation of children's and adolescents' rights and responsibilities and what the law requires. Training also requires dealing with children's assumptions and misconceptions about abductions and how to become empowered as reporters of victimizations.

SOME SUGGESTIONS FOR EFFECTIVELY ACCOMPLISHING TRAINING GOALS

Children's Cognitive Maturity

Children's level of cognitive development must be taken into consideration. For example, prior to adolescence, children need to be provided with concrete examples, not hypothetical, theoretical situations, in order for them to accurately grasp a concept. Thus, permitting children to watch a videotape of a potential abduction, depicting a child the same age as the viewers, would be a helpful tool in the curriculum training program. Behavioral rehearsal (see chapter 5) is also recommended for younger children: having children role play positive solutions to conflict situations that are presented to them in the classroom setting. Paula Geonie, founder and president of Playing It Safe, recommends behavioral rehearsal for young children with the assistance of puppets—what she refers to as "puppet pals" that role play vignettes related to potential abductions, including walking home alone from school, answering the door when children are home alone, and so on.

Susan Newman (1985), in *Never Say Yes to a Stranger*, includes photographs of each step in a scenario depicting a potential abduction. For example, in a situation described as "Which Way to the Police Station," Newman shows photographs of a young boy walking alone, a man motioning to the boy to come to his car, the boy going to the man's car, and so on. A story line accompanies each of the photographs, and a series of questions and alternative answers are provided at the end of the scenario.

Older children and adolescents may rely more on scenarios that require them to answer a series of questions concerning positive and negative responses to conflict, attitudes and feelings of children who are confronted with a potential abduction, and strategies for reporting children's experiences to parents, teachers, and law enforcement personnel. Examples of this type of pedagogical technique are the following:

Scenario

Suzy is a girl in the fifth grade, just like you are. She lives in ———. A few blocks from Suzy's house there is a beautiful park. Suzy and her friends meet in the playground in the park almost every day after school. One day Suzy and her friends saw a man walking toward them. Suzy saw that this man was carrying a dog leash. "Can you help me find my little puppy?" asked the man. "I think she ran into the park. I miss her so much. Can you help me find her?" the man said. Suzy felt sorry for this man who had lost his puppy. The man told her, "Your mommy and daddy will be really proud of you if you help me find my lost dog." The man then started hugging Suzy and asked her again to help him find his puppy.

Questions Following the Reading of the Scenario

1. What do you think Suzy should have done when the man started talking to her?

2. Do you think Suzy should have talked to the man?

3. Do you think Suzy should go help the man find the puppy? Why or why not?

4. Would you help the man find his puppy? Why or why not?

5. How do you think Suzy felt when the man started hugging her?

6. What do you think Suzy should do when she goes home to her parents?

7. Do you think Suzy's parents would want her to go with this man? Why or why not?

8. How can we keep Suzy safe from this man?

Scenario

Mike went to the shopping mall with his dad. On the way out of the mall, Mike saw a parked motorcycle. He left his dad and went over to look at the motorcycle. Mike checked out the dials on the dashboard. He looked over the motor and looked at the owner's helmet that was sitting on top of the seat. In a few minutes, the owner of the motorcycle came over to Mike and said, "Hi. This is my bike. Do you like it? What's your name?" Mike told him his name. And then the owner said, "Want to ride on my bike with me?" "How about a quick ride—just around the parking lot. We'll have fun. I'm your friend. Your dad won't care."

Questions Following the Reading of the Scenario

1. Do you think Mike should have left his father in the parking lot? Why or why not?

2. Do you think Mike should have left the motorcycle when the owner appeared?

3. Would you go for a ride on the motorcycle or go back to your father? Why?

4. Do you think the owner of the motorcycle is Mike's friend? What do you think a friend is?

5. Do you think Mike's father would care if Mike went for a ride on the motorcycle?

6. If you were with Mike, what would you tell him about the owner of the motorcycle?

7. How can we keep Mike safe from the owner of the motorcycle?

Establishing an Atmosphere of Trust

In addition to taking into consideration the children's level of cognitive maturity, curriculum projects must make it a priority to accomplish the goals of the training without creating undue anxiety for children and teens. Trainers must be able to relate well to a variety of children, so that the children will feel comfortable talking with them and listening to them about the legal and psychological issues involved. Trainers also must be able to discuss sexuality and deviant behavior without blushing, passing judgment, or exhibiting signs of disapproval. Trainers must be fair and candid when dealing with questions without permitting personal feelings to interfere with effectiveness. Trainers must establish rapport and a respectful atmosphere in training sessions, in which feelings of anger, confusion, fear, and mistrust can be expressed without fear of being ridiculed or retaliated against. This is especially true for trainers working with young children.

Ensuring Support Outside of the Classroom

Inviting parents, members of the school board, and other concerned individuals to participate in the curriculum projects can ensure support outside the classroom. Several organizations may be contacted for participation in the programs, even to the extent of teaching a module in an area pertinent to their expertise. Examples of these organizations include the police force, American Association of University Women, YMCA, YWCA, Girl Scouts, Girls Club, and Boys Club. Trainers should work with any interested parents on ways to reinforce the messages of the curriculum project at home (also see chapter 5). For example, Paula Geonie, as part of her Playing It Safe program, includes "safety songs" that have as their goal reminding children of the information they were taught about strangers, safety, reporting, and so on.

EDUCATIONAL QUALIFICATIONS OF TRAINERS

In addition to the personality factors we raised above the following educational qualifications should also be evaluated by any school district seeking a trainer in child abductions and missing children:

1. Knowledge of psychological theories of sexual abuse and of power, which is helpful when training students in abductions and victimization. Trainers must be able to explain psychological terms in nontechnical language for children.

2. Knowledge of child and adolescent development, including cognitive development, personality development, development of emotions, such as fear and anger.

3. Knowledge of research and theories on gender-role socialization. This knowledge must include socialization agents—parents, peers, media, teachers, music—theories of gender-role acquisition, and research on verbal and nonverbal communication skills.

4. Knowledge of recent case law and legislation.

5. Fluency in languages in addition to English (or have a co-trainer who can meet this need).

It is recommended that trainers be interviewed in person by a few individuals who represent the group of individuals for whom the training will be provided. Areas of inquiry include the following:

1. Education/training in the psychological issues involved in abduction and missing children.

2. Education/training in the legal issues involved in this area.

3. Publications/presentations on the topic.

4. List of previous training seminars/workshops and individuals who can give recommendations about previous training programs.

5. Outlines and/or video tapes of previous training seminars/workshops.

6. Familiarity with children and schools.

7. Ability to work with teachers, parents, adminstrators, and school-board members.

8. Education/training in psychological issues involved in facilitating a training program.

POST-TRAINING FACTORS TO CONSIDER

Consideration must be given to the following prior to the initiation of any training program:

1. What provisions does our school have for children whose wish to report an experience was prompted by the training?

2. Do we have trained child and/or school psychologists available during and following the training session to assist any childen who have "flashbacks" or are visibly upset after the training?

3. Have we obtained parental permission for this training program?

4. Do we have contacts with law-enforcement personnel who can assist us with children's reports of experiences that are prompted by the training program?

5. What follow-up to the training programs do we have in place?

6. How often will the training programs be offered?

7. What means of reinforcing the information from the training program have we instituted (e.g., projects with parents)?

PSYCHOLOGICAL ISSUES TO CONSIDER WHEN CONDUCTING TRAINING PROGRAMS

One of the repeated findings from research and training programs at schools concerns the resistance to talking about abductions. These experiences are difficult to discuss. Resolutions may seem out of reach and burdensome, and the behaviors are occurring to someone we know or to our-selves at the time we are participating in a training program. While we may want to avoid discussing child abductions and abuse, we have little choice since child abductions are reaching epidemic proportions. It is a topic that must be addressed.

Questions that dominate the training sessions tend to be classified as those that deal with the nature of abduc-tions and abuse and those that reflect a frustration about the topic. Children's and adolescents' questions reflect fear and confusion surrounding abductions. The topic of ab-ductions arouses discomfort and defensiveness. Adolescents may want to joke about abuse. Would they joke that way in a training program on racial relations or AIDS? Most likely not. Training sessions on abductions inevitably chal-lenge widely held assumptions about female-male relation-ships and power that are not easy to change. Some older children and adolescents may joke during the training ses-sion as a coping strategy.

It is important to give legitimacy to the anxieties, con-fusion, and fears raised by participants in the training pro-grams. In addition, it is necessary to establish rapport and a respectful atmosphere in the training session. It is also impor-tant to talk openly about the attitudes individuals bring with them to the session, perhaps using the issues raised in national media accounts as an example of an abduction (e.g., Adam Walsh, Sara Anne Wood) as a starting point.

It is imperative that trainers as well as school admin-istrators know that some children may be experiencing sexual abuse and that the anger they feel toward the perpetrator may be expressed to the trainer. Guidance counselors must be present during training programs to assist in this regard.

SAMPLE CURRICULA

The following lesson plans are geared for a two-class-period presentation. Suggestions for topics are offered both for elemen-tary and for secondary school students.

Lesson 1. Introduction to Program and Definitions

(1 class period)

Objectives

At the conclusion of this class, students will be able to

1. Assess their own perceptions of child abductions and

2. Adequately label behaviors as illustrative of abductions or not illustrative of abductions.

Introduction

For Secondary School Students
Trainer welcomes students to class.
Trainer introduces her- or himself to students.
Students introduce themselves and state one question they want to have answered in training sessions or tell trainer what they believe a "stranger" is like.
Trainer writes these answers on the flipchart/chalkboard for all students to see.
Trainer summarizes students' responses.
Trainer states goals for training session.

For Elementary School Students
Trainer welcomes students to class.
Trainer introduces her- or himself to students.
Students introduce themselves and tell trainer what they believe a "stranger" is like.
Trainer states goals for training session.

Definitions of "Missing" Children and Child Abductions

For Secondary School Students
Trainer distributes copies of a case study (see above discussion).
Students read case study to answer trainer-directed questions.
Trainer lectures and leads guided discussion of abductions:

Who is a stranger?
What kinds of children get abducted?
Noncustodial parental abductions.
Runaways.
Trainer asks questions about content—verbally or in written quiz form.
Trainer makes summary comments from this unit.
Trainer asks for questions or comments.

For Elementary School Students
Trainer distributes copies of case study.
Students read case study to answer trainer-directed questions.
Trainer lectures and leads guided discussion of abductions.
Trainer makes summary comments from this unit.
Trainer posts major points from lesson
Trainer identifies goals of next class period.
Trainer asks for questions or comments.

Lesson 2. Avoiding a Potential Abductor

(1 class period)

Objectives

At the conclusion of this class, students will be able to

1. determine action to take if a person experiences a potential abduction,

2. determine solutions to incidents of potential abductions,

3. examine the school's policy on abductions and missing children,

4. summarize major issues in child abductions identified in two class periods.

For Secondary School Students
Presentation
    Knowing full name, address, and phone number
    Knowing how to dial 911 or 0
    Establishing a codeword or codephrase

Avoding monogramed articles
Avoiding unconditional affection
Challenging adult authority
Run, yell, and tell
Behavioral Rehearsal
Approach by a stranger while walking home from class
Approach by a stranger at the door while at home alone
Trainer will review information from previous two classes by using flipchart/chalkboard.
Trainer will announce goals of final class period devoted to abductions.
Trainer asks students to list ways they can work with their school in preventing abductions.
Trainer asks students to list ways they can work with their parents in preventing abductions.
Trainer posts these responses on the flipchart/chalkboard.
Trainer distributes copies of school's policy statement on abductions.
Trainer introduces individual charged with implementing policy statement (optional).
Trainer leads guided discussion of policy statement.
Trainer asks students to list additional educational programs for their school.
Trainer reviews major points from two class periods Trainer asks students to reread case study and answer questions.
Trainer meets individually with students who wish to speak privately.

For Elementary School Students
Presentation
Knowing full name, address, and phone number
Knowing how to dial 911 or 0
Establishing a codeword or codephrase
Avoiding monogramed articles
Avoiding unconditional affection
Challenging adult authority
Run, yell, and tell

Behavioral Rehearsal
   Approach by a stranger while walking on a playground
   Approach by a stranger at the door while at home with
      a babysitter
Trainer will review information from previous class by using
   flipchart/chalkboard
Trainer will announce goals of final class period devoted to
   abductions.
Trainer asks students to list ways they can work with their
   school in preventing abductions.
Trainer asks students to list ways they can work with their
   parents in preventing abductions.
Trainer posts these responses on the flipchart/chalkboard.
Trainer distributes copies of school's policy statement on ab-
   ductions for students' parents.
Trainer introduces individual charged with implementing policy
   statement (optional).
Trainer asks students to reread case study and answer questions.
Trainer meets individually with students who wish to speak
   privately.

ADDITIONAL RESPONSIBILITIES
OF SCHOOLS

In addition to faciliating training programs for children and
adolescents, school districts may want to consider the following programs to meet their mission of providing education on
child abductions and missing children:

1. information-based seminars for school personnel concerning myths and realities of abductions (see chapter 1) and
   the school's responsibility for reporting missing children;

2. information-based presentations for parents concerning
   the school's active role in preventing missing children
   and abductions;

3. development of brochures, pamphlets, and posters de-
   scribing the school's efforts in preventing abductions
   and in educating all members of the school's community in avoidance strategies;

4. development of study-time activities, tutoring, and rec-
    reation before and after school so that students do not
    have to be home alone;

5. development of a school callback program so that when
    a student does not arrive to school as scheduled, vol-
    unteers at the school call the student's parent(s) to make
    sure the absence is excused;

6. information-based Child Safety Awareness Week—in-
    vite law-enforcement personnel and legislators to give
    presentations to children and parents;

7. encourage teachers to incorporate discussions of miss-
    ing children in other courses, such as reading, social
    studies, and English.

SUMMARY

In this chapter we have offered some recommendations for training programs for children and adolescents that
have, as their major focus, ways to empower the students to
take control of their bodies and actions. Certainly, the suggestions offered here will not be the cure-all for the problem
of abductions and missing children. However, it is an important beginning for schools to take responsibility for caring
for and educating children. A systematic and continuous
focus on the concepts offered by training programs in schools
and in the home will help children and adolescents become
less vulnerable to victimization. Since the abductor's prime
victim is a child or adolescent naive to safety strategies,
educating students will make the abductor's job of luring
them more difficult. In concert with education by parents
and teachers, legislative action must be taken in the areas of
education/training, stiffer penalties for abductors and abusers, and counseling programs for families of missing children. It is to this issue, federal and state legislation, that we
turn in the next chapter.

REFERENCE

Newman, S. (1985). *Never Say Yes to a Stranger*. New York: Perigee.

IIII 7

The Role and Responsibilities of Legislators in Protecting and Assisting Children

INTRODUCTION

In 1994, New York State Senator Dean Skelos and Assembly-member James Tedisco released detailed information on legislative proposals they had designed to address the issue of missing and exploited children. They announced this ten-bill package to residents of the state on Valentine's Day, a day they believed appropriate since it is a day recognized for love and affection. The child protection program they proposed had, as its main goal, ways to diminish child abductions and ensure swift and certain punishment for criminals who exploit and victimize children.

Their package was highlighted by a mandatory school curriculum bill that requires abduction prevention training in elementary schools. This bill was approved both by the Assembly and by the Senate and signed into law by former Governor Mario Cuomo. The package also included proposals that would

1. require certain sex offenders to register with state and local criminal-justice officials upon prison release or change of address;

2. require police and other officials to "flag" state and local birth and school records to help track abductors;

3. require schools to obtain additional information about parents and abductors;

4   require central reporting of all child abduction cases and missing child reports in the state;

5.   require school officials to notify parents within three hours of the start of classes in the case of unauthorized school absence;

6.   increase penalties for noncustodial parent abductions;

7.   make it a felony for an adult to assist a minor child in running away from custodial parents;

8.   reduce the waiting period for families victimized by child abduction to be eligible for counseling services;

9.   ensure that any felony defendant who is found not responsible for reason of mental illness serve the same time in a mental institution that he or she would have served if convicted of the felony as charged in the indictment.

Senator Skelos and Assemblymember Tedisco wanted to show children and adolescents in New York State that their safety is one of the top priorities in the legislature. They also believe that there is no better legacy to leave to New York State than to advocate as law-makers for changes to protect the lives of future resources. Other legislators across the country share their sentiment and bring to their work in the state legislatures their vast experience as parents, teachers, attorneys, civil-rights activists and their commitment to bettering the lives of children. This chapter summarizes the legislation on child abductions and missing children that exists in the United States.

MISSING CHILDREN: FEDERAL LEGISLATION

In the 1980s, the problem of missing children emerged into our national consciousness, fueled by the following events:

1.   the abduction and disappearance of Etan Patz in New York City in 1979;

2. the establishment of Child Find of America, Incorporated, in New York City in 1980; and

3. John Walsh, father of murdered child, Adam Walsh, became a national spokesperson for advocating change in legislation on missing children in 1981.

These events highlighted the need for political attention and legislation. In 1982, then Florida Senator Paula Hawkins and Illinois Congressperson Paul Simon led the way for important legislation to protect children. Specifically, the United States Senate declared May 25 National Missing Children's Day and Congress passed the Missing Children Act of 1982, which authorized the FBI to enter as well as maintain information about missing persons in the National Crime Information Center.

In addition, the U.S. Congress also passed the Missing Children's Assistance Act of 1984, which was reauthorized in 1988 and in 1992. This law requires the Office of Juvenile Justice and Deliquency Prevention in the United States Department of Justice to

1. create a national, toll-free telephone line to receive reports of sightings of missing children and to assist in reuniting such children with their families;

2. create a national resource center and clearinghouse to provide technical assistance to those seeking to locate and recover missing children; and

3. monitor contracts and grants to public agencies and private nonprofit agencies for activities in prevention, location, and recovery of missing children and research into the causes of missing children.

The National Center for Missing and Exploited Children serves as the national resource center and operates the national hotline (see appendix B).

The U.S. Congress passed the National Child Search Assistance Act in 1990. This law requires each federal, state, and local law-enforcement agency to report each case of a missing child (anyone under 18) to the National Center for Missing and Exploited Children. Furthermore, this law states that no agency is to maintain any policy establishing a waiting period before accepting reports on missing children or unidentified persons. Each agency must immediately enter identifying information about the child or adolescent, which can be supplemented within sixty days with any other information, including dental and medical records. Law enforcement agencies are required to maintain close contact with the National Center for Missing and Exploited Children for exchange of identifying information.

MISSING CHILDREN: STATE LEGISLATION

To supplement this federal legislation, comprehensive state legislation has been proposed throughout the United States that further protects children from abductions. Several issues have been addressed through state legislation, including

1. a waiting period for investigation,

2. maintaining files of unidentified persons,

3. cross checking of school records,

4. flagging of school records,

5. verification of student absences, and

6. counseling for families.

We will summarize each of these areas in which legislation has been proposed at the state level.

Waiting Period for Investigation

One problem with missing children cases is that official action is delayed because of twenty-four-, forty-eight-, or seventy-two-hour waiting periods before an investigation is undertaken. These waiting periods were commonly established in the hope that children or teens would "turn up" or return home to their families within a few hours or days, thus making an official search unnecessary. This belief that children turn up soon has not been supported by statistics throughout the United States, however. In the majority of states, there is now no waiting period prior to an investigation. This ensures that precious hours are not lost before conducting an investigation. Children can be in a different county or even a different state in a few hours. It is thus imperative to begin a search immediately upon notification that a child or teen is missing.

Maintaining Files of Unidentified Persons

The Missing Children's Act of 1982 provides for a nationwide tracking system to address the problem of unidentified persons who are mentally incapacitated or deceased. The National Center for Missing and Exploited Children attempts to identify the more than two thousand children who are currently identified as "Jane Doe" or "John Doe" in the FBI files. State legislators have recognized the importance of assisting the federal government in this tracking system. Several states have enacted legislation that would establish a centralized file of information to identify missing children. However, it should be noted that many of these files are not compatible with the National Crime Information Center files. They thus do not achieve the main goal of national coordinated efforts. This problem calls for further legislation.

Cross Checking of School Records

In Ohio, the names of all newly enrolled and transferred school students and children in day care facilities were sent to its state clearinghouse for missing persons so as to make a comparison with the roster of missing children. Approximately four hundred missing children were located through the use of this technique. When enrollment records are computerized and centralized, such a procedure for locating children is manageable. In the state of California, the principal of each school that a child enters or to which the child transfers, is urged to check to determine whether the child's identifying information resembles that of any child listed as missing in the bulletins provided by the state department of justice. In four states—Montana, Nevada, Ohio, and

Virginia—schools are required to contact the missing children clearinghouse and local law-enforcement personnel should a parent not provide a birth certificate or information from the last school the child attended.

Flagging of School Records

Several states require law enforcement agencies to notify state record-keeping agencies and schools when a child is listed as missing. The agency or school is then required to flag the child's records and notify the law-enforcement agency immediately should a request be received for the child's records. Such requests are common, especially when a child is abducted by a noncustodial parent who wants to enroll his or her child in school or day care. However, the abductors' requests do not prevent further flight on the part of the abductor.

Verification of Student Absences

In New York State, schools are required to advise parents that they have the right to be notified if their daughter or son fails to attend school as expected. In Rhode Island and Virginia, school attendance staff are required to contact the student's parents or guardians when the school has not been advised of the pupil's absence. Such a program is urgent, given the statistics that suggest that many children are abducted on their way to and from school. Those states that do have this call-back program also have provisions to exempt the school from any liability if the school is unable, after reasonable efforts, to notify the parent or guardian of the child's absence.

Counseling for Families

In New York State, legislation became enacted in 1995 that permits the availability of psychotherapeutic counseling within one week of a suspected abduction for members of the child's or adolescent's families. Family members frequently report many of the same emotional symptoms as expressed by abductees (see Chapter 1). Families are encouraged to seek counseling through referrals from the Crime Victims Board.

STATE CLEARINGHOUSES

Clearinghouses are important resources in solving cases of missing children. A clearinghouse is a central point for law-enforcement personnel, education programs, prevention programs, and legislators to coordinate their efforts in locating abducted and missing children and teens. The National Center for Missing and Exploited Children recommends the following functions of clearinghouses:

1. collecting and maintaining computerized data and investigative information on missing persons in the state;

2. compiling statistics on the missing children's cases handled and the number resolved by the clearinghouse each year;

3. assisting in the training of law enforcement and other professionals on issues relating to missing and unidentified persons;

4. operating a clearinghouse of information regarding prevention of abduction and sexual exploitation of children;

5. keeping and distributing information regarding methods of locating and recovering missing persons;

6. assisting in the preparation and dissemination of flyers of missing persons and their abductors;

7. publishing, on a regular basis, a directory of missing persons for dissemination to state and local public and nonprofit agencies and to the public;

8. establishing and operating a statewide, toll-free telephone line for reports of missing persons and reports of sightings of missing persons.

In New York State, a statewide Missing and Exploited Children Clearinghouse within the Division of Criminal Justice Services has been operating since 1987. The staff of the clearinghouse interacts with schools as well as community-based organizations to develop education and prevention programs concerning child safety. In addition, staff, with appropriate

parental consent, duplicate photographs and posters of children reported missing by local police and disseminate this information throughout the state through the media, law
enforcement, and publicity programs. The clearinghouse staff
also establish a case database containing nonidentifying facts
and statistics relative to missing and exploited children cases.
The data are profiled to assist law-enforcement personnel with
their investigations of child abductions.

In 1988, the U.S. Congress authorized the Office of
Juvenile Justice and Delinquency Prevention to award grants
to establish and operate clearinghouses. Forty-three states have
created state clearinghouses for missing children.

LEGISLATION DEALING WITH
PREVENTION OF CHILD ABDUCTIONS
AND MISSING CHILDREN

In addition to legislation on waiting periods, cross check of
school records and verification of student absences, it has been
recognized that legislation must deal with preventative measures, especially the screening of child-care personnel. In this
section we will summarize the following preventative issues:

1. screening of individuals providing services to children,

2. licensing of child-care facilities,

3. criminal history information,

4. registration of sex offenders, and

5. mandatory prison sentences for sex offenders.

Screening of Individuals Providing
Services to Children

According to the National Center for Missing and Exploited
Children, screening of personnel, especially in child-care facilities, is required in most states for current staff and new appli-
cants. However, to date there is no uniformity on a national
level on the language of the statutes requiring screening of
personnel working with children. Some states do include juvenile detention and correction personnel and foster-care work-

ers in their definition of child care-personnel. Some states include volunteer as well as employed staff in their definition. Uniformity in language as well as categories of personnel is urgently needed legislation.

Licensing of Child Care Facilities

The majority of state statues do provide for inspection of physical facilities and screening for health problems and prior convictions of personnel. Some states have also provided for training programs for individuals working with children.

The National Center for Missing and Exploited Children recommends that the following issues should be supported by a state child-care facility statue:

1. licensing of family child-care locations as well as daycare facilities;

2. licensing of residential as well as day programs;

3. screening of volunteers and prospective and current employees;

4. screening of family members who may be present on a regular basis at a family child-care facility;

5. regular reviews of the license;

6. procedures and rules governing the denial or suspension of a license and administrative review of the denial;

7. training of all personnel in first aid, recognition, and prevention of communicable diseases and recognition and prevention of child abuse;

8. the development of procedures for receiving, investigating, and preserving records of complaints of child maltreatment made against individual child-care providers.

Criminal History Information

Federal laws have been enacted requiring criminal-history checks to be conducted. State laws to this effect have also been enacted. The National Center for Missing and Exploited Children recommends that a criminal-history check be a two-part process:

1. a check through the state law-enforcement information system to determine if there have been any particular kinds of offenses committed by that individual in the state; and

2. a check through the FBI's National Crime Information Center Interstate Identification Index to determine if other states have records of the criminal history of the individual.

As a result of the provisions the United States Congress included in the Victims of Child Abuse Act of 1990, all individuals working with children in federal facilities are required to have background checks. Some states require certain employers to request a check of public safety records of all available convictions involving sex crimes of individuals who apply for employment or for a volunteer position involving working with children. In other states, broader criminal records checks must be conducted. In many states, the penalties for failure to disclose information of previous arrests or convictions is included on the background check application form.

Registration of Sex Offenders

Some states have legislated specific provisions to guarantee more protection for children, considering the fact that most abductors are repeat offenders. Only a few states require the institution from which an offender is to be released to give notice to all police departments and district attorneys' offices throughout the state. The National Center for Missing and Exploited Children recommends that state statues with regard to registration of sex offenders do the following:

1. require lifetime registration;

2. require registration within ten days of assuming residence in a new community;

3. prohibit public inspection of registry information which should be accessible only by law-enforcement personnel or other individuals authorized by law;

4. require the offender to appear in person to register with local law enforcement;

5. establish penalties for failure to comply with the provisions of the registry.

Mandatory Prison Sentences for Sex Offenders

There are some states that have already enacted legislation that provides for mandatory prison sentences for those convicted of certain sexual crimes against children. In North Carolina, for example, individuals convicted of a sexual offense with a child younger than thirteen, receive mandatory life imprisonment. In Missouri, mandatory imprisonment is instituted for any subsequent conviction for incest, abuse of a child, use of a child in sexual performance, or promotion of a sexual performance by a child.

A CALL TO ACTION

In this chapter we have summarized the federal and state legislation currently enacted that deals with child-centered and abductor-centered issues. Throughout the chapter lies a common thread: that more legislation is needed to deal with missing children and child abductions. Legislators need the guidance and support of their constituents in this regard. A very powerful tool for constituents to use to convey their opinion, support, or opposition to bills dealing with missing children, is lobbying. Lobbyists are individuals or groups of individuals who provide members of state assemblies and senates with information that might otherwise not be available to them. In New York State, for example, Missing and Exploited Children Clearinghouse advises the senate and assembly regarding the creation or modification of laws that relate to the issue of missing and exploited children. The goals of lobbying—in person or in writing—are to inform and to persuade. John Walsh's lobbying efforts have been successful in establishing federal laws. In the introduction to the National Center for Missing and Exploited Children's *Guide for Effective State Laws to Protect Children,* 1993, he stated:

> In the years since my son, Adam, was abducted and murdered, I have traveled all across this country to advocate for changes in the system. The only way I have found to make meaningful and permanent change is to work through the system. One of the most effective ways is to change laws. The quality of a child's life in the legal, education, criminal justice, and social services systems varies greatly from state to state. Therefore we need to begin our work in each of the state legislatures if we are to make significant change. (xiii)

In the Appendices to this book we have listed several ways you can join John Walsh in making significant change.

REFERENCE

National Center for Missing and Exploited Children (1993). *Selected State Legislation: A Guide for Effective State Laws to Protect Children.* Arlington, VA: Author.

Epilogue

As we have pointed out throughout this book, the problem of child abductions and missing children is one that deeply affects every aspect of our society, from the family to the school to the governing bodies of our states. In this light we have offered suggestions for parents, teachers, and legislators to take preventative and educational measures to maximize the safety of children and adolescents. But the problem of missing children and child abductions is a societal problem. All of us—even if we are not parents, teachers, or elected officials—must watch out for children and teens and be additional deterrants to abductors. For example, if we see an individual in a car pulled up to talk to children, we must intervene—ask if there is a problem; offer to give directions ourselves; see that children return home safely; report the occurrence to parents and police, should the children feel uncomfortable about what the individual said to them.

Children are everyone's responsibility. They are our hope for the future. We must all treat them as our greatest resource. They should not be treated as hobbies, but as individuals in their own right. We must decenter from our own perspectives and life stages and recognize the needs and rights of children and adolescents. We need to value childhood and adolescence; to regard these periods as important stages of the life span to which children and teens are entitled. When we rear children and adolescents with greater security and with higher self-esteem, they will be at lesser risk of abductions.

We must offer our hands and our help to those children and adolescents who need us.

Appendices

Appendix A
Recommendations for Future Research on Missing Children and Child Abductions

INTRODUCTION

As we have pointed out in this book, the size of the problem of missing children and child abductions is enormous and their impact is serious. Research needs in this field are vast as well as urgent. Individuals who testify as expert witnesses must have reliable and valid data from methodologically sound studies on which to base their opinions. Furthermore, an increase in research in the field of missing children will enhance the quality of the treatment methods for the child and teen victims themselves as well as for their family members and friends. Funding sources for researchers must acknowledge the importance of studying missing children. Funds for in-depth, controlled studies must be made available from granting institutions.

We offer the following suggestions for future research in this field and recommend this research be conducted by scientists in several disciplines in collaboration with each other, including developmental psychologists, sociologists, child educators, family therapists, and criminologists. Some sample references for research purposes is also presented in these Appendices.

RESEARCH RECOMMENDATIONS

To date, little or no attention has been focused on the way in which children themselves define, conceptualize, or label their victimization experiences. How a child or adolescent defines or labels the situation may determine the extent and direction of her or his help-seeking behaviors. Thus, asking the victim to define her or his experiences will guide research questions.

Research on abductors and abusers has typically examined a variety of excuses for this violence, including prior victimization, use of violent pornography, and alcohol abuse. Research must view abductions as intentional behavior designed to achieve the goals of the assailant.

Research on missing children must not view these children as homogeneous but diverse on a variety of variables, including age, sex, class, race, and ethnicity. Each of these variables provides an additional context to the violence that must be identified and interpreted as we attempt to better understand the abductions experienced by children and adolescents.

Researchers, legislators, and law-enforcement personnel must have comprehensive, annual, national and state figures on all forms of missing children that are supplemented by regular national studies. The Uniform Crime Reports, for example, has made no age information available about victimizations, with the exception of homicides. Statistics must be compiled so that information can be aggregated nationally and compared across states.

The radiating impact of child abductions must be addressed. Family members of the victim often struggle with issues of disclosure, confrontation, and religion. Research must address the impact of this type of victimization on family and friends, in terms of somatic and psychological outcomes.

Additional research into the emotional reactions in the aftermath of an abduction must be conducted. Variables to consider in this research include panic attacks and agoraphobia, learned helplessness, emotional denial, body image problems, intimacy and sexuality problems, and self-destructive behaviors.

Research on perpetrators must include in its definition parents and other family members. Research has typically relied on "strangers" as perpetrators, despite the incidence of children's, especially young children's, experiences with intrafamily abduction and victimization.

Research must document children's strategies for victimization avoidance that are appropriate at different stages of their development.

Research must also be conducted on teens who run away from foster homes as well as those who run away from their families of origin.

Researchers must focus their attention on same-sex adult-child victimization as well as other sex perpetrator-victim relationships.

Finally, attention must be paid to the context of data collection in research on child abductions and missing children, such as the match of sex between child or adolescent and the interviewer, in order to obtain more accurate information. Some children may be reluctant to discuss their victimization experiences with an other-sex researcher.

Appendix B
Missing Children and Child Abductions: Resources for Advocacy

HOTLINES

Child Find	1-800-431-5005
National Child Safety Council	1-800-222-1464
National Center for Missing Children	1-800-843-5678
National Runaway Hotline	1-800-621-4000
Runaway Hotline	1-800-231-6946
Missing and Exploited Children Clearinghouse	1-800-346-3543
Hope Eating Disorders Program	1-800-635-1022
Drug-Abuse Information	1-800-522-5353
National Recovery Institutes	1-800-262-2946
Eating Disorder Center	1-800-541-3733
Women's Therapeutic Services	1-800-833-4087
AIDS Prevention Hotline	1-800-541-2437

ORGANIZATIONS

Abducted Children Information Center
1470 Gene St.
Winter Park, FL 32789

Adam Walsh Child Resource Center, Inc.
1876 North University Dr.
Fort Lauderdale, FL 33322

131

Parents against Child Snatching
5554 Cobb Meadow
Norcross, GA 30093

Parents of Murdered Children
1739 Bella Vista
Cincinnati, OH 45237

Child Find
P.O. Box 277
New Paltz, NY 12561

Family Violence Research and Treatment Program
1310 Clinic Dr.
Tyler, TX 75701

National Clearinghouse on Child Abuse and Neglect
P.O. Box 1182
Washington, DC 20013

National Legal Resource Center for Child Advocacy
   and Protection
American Bar Association
1800 M St. NW
Washington, DC 20036

Women against Pornography
358 W. 47th St.
New York, NY 10036

Stop Sexual Abuse of Children
Chicago Public Education Project
American Friends Service Committee
407 Dearborn St.
Chicago, IL 60605

Alliance against Sexual Coercion
P.O. Box 1
Cambridge, MA 02139

National Center for Prosecution of Child Abuse
1033 N. Fairfax St. Suite 200
Alexandria, VA 22314

Sexual Assault Recovery through Awareness and Hope
P.O. Box 20353
Bradenton, FL 34203

Survivors of Incest Anonymous
P.O. Box 21817
Baltimore, MD 21222

People against Sexual Abuse
26 Court Street Suite 315
Brooklyn, NY 11242

American Psychological Association
750 First St. NE
Washington, DC 20002

American Anorexia and Bulimia Association
133 Cedar Lane
Teaneck, NJ 07666

Alcoholics Anonymous
Box 459
Grand Central Station
New York, NY 10163

Johns Hopkins Eating and Weight Disorders Clinic
600 North Wolfe St.
Baltimore, MD 21205

Mothers of AIDS Patients
1811 Field Dr. NE
Albuquerqe, NM 87112

American Disability Association
2121 Eighth Ave.
Birmingham, AL 35203

American Association of Sex Educators, Counselors,
   and Therapists
11 Dupont Circle
Washington, DC 20036

Sex Information and Education Council of the United States
84 Fifth Avenue
New York, NY 10011

Information Service of the Kinsey Institute for Sex Research
Indiana University
Bloomington, IN 47401

Bureau of Venereal Disease Control
New York City Health Department
93 Worth St.
New York, NY 10013

Appendix C
Missing Children and Child Abductions: Resources for Education

RESOURCES FOR RESEARCH ON MISSING CHILDREN AND CHILD ABDUCTIONS

Sample Listing of Journals

American Psychologist
Child Abuse and Neglect
Journal of Traumatic Stress
American Journal of Diseases of Children
Violence and Victims
Journal of Quantitative Criminology
Journal of Interpersonal Violence
Victimology
Psychological Bulletin
Crime and Delinquency
Journal of Primary Prevention
Journal of Child and Family Studies
Victimology: An International Journal
Journal of Family Violence
Sexual Coercion and Assault
Children and Society
Journal of Comparative Family Studies
Journal of Psychiatry and Law
Child and Adolescent Social Work Journal
Journal of Family Psychology
Journal of Child Sexual Abuse

American Journal of Orthopsychiatry
Cinical Pediatrics
Family and Conciliation Courts Reivew
Law and Human Behavior
Early Child Development and Care
Psychology in the Schools

RESOURCES FOR LOCATING MATERIAL ON CHILD ABDUCTIONS AND MISSING CHILDREN

Indexes and Abstracts

Educational Resources Information Center (ERIC)
Psychological Abstracts
Current Index to Journals in Education
Social Science Index
Sociological Abstracts
Women's Studies Abstracts
Crime Victims Digest
National Crime Survey
Uniform Crime Reports

Federal Government

Department of Health and Human Services
Federal Bureau of Investigation
Department of Justice

Sample Textbooks

Best, J. (1990). *Threatened Children: Rhetoric and Concern about Child Victims.* Chicago: University of Chicago Press.

Eth, S., and R. Pynoos. (1985). *Post-Traumatic Stress Disorder in Children.* Washington: American Psychiatric Press.

Greven, P. (1990). *Spare the Child: the Religious Roots of Punishment and the Psychological Impact of Physical Abuse.* New York: Knopf.

Hyman, I. (1990). *Reading Writing and the Hickory Stick: The Appaling Story of Physical and Psychological Abuse in American Schools.* Lexington, MA: Lexington Books.

Patton, M. (1991). *Family Sexual Abuse: Frontline Research and Evaluation.* Newbury Park, CA: Sage.

Star, R., and D. Wolfe (eds.). (1991). *The Effects of Child Abuse and Neglect: Issues and Research.* New York: Guilford.

Straus, M., and R. Gelles. (1990). *Physical Violence in American Families: Risk Factors and Adaptations in 8,145 Families.* New Brunswick, NJ: Transaction.

Sample Data Sources

Bureau of Justice Statistics. (1991). *Teenage Victims: A National Crime Survey Report* (NCJ-128129). Washington, DC: U.S. Department of Justice.

———. (1992). *Criminal Victimization in the United States, 1900: A National Crime Victimization Survey Report* (NCJ-134126). Washington, DC: U.S. Department of Justice.

Federal Bureau of Investigation. (1992). *Crime in the United States, 1991: Uniform Crime Reports.* Washington, DC: U.S. Department of Justice.

National Center on Child Abuse and Neglect. (1992). *National Child Abuse and Neglect Data System* (working paper no. 1): *1990 Summary Data Component* (DHHS publication no. ACF 92-30361). Washington, DC: Department of Health and Human Services.

SEMINARS/MOTIVATIONAL SPEAKERS AND INSTRUCTION KITS

Becoming Streetwise: A Guide to Personal Safety
Target Consultants International Ltd.
P.O. Box 463
Massapequa Park, NY 11762

Playing It Safe
123 Eileen Way
Syosset, NY 11791

My Personal Safety Coloring Book
Fridley Police Department
6431 University Avenue, NE
Fridley, MN 55432

National School Safety Center
4165 Thousand Oaks Blvd. Suite 290
Westlake Village, CA 91362

Protecting Our Loved Ones International
P.O. Box 150058
San Rafael, CA 94915

SAMPLE VIDEOS

Child Abuse: Stop the Hurt (for the hearing impaired)
D.S.S. Deaf Access Office
744 P. Street
M.S. 15-10
Sacremento, CA 95814

Incest: The Family Secret
Filmmakers Library
124 E. 40th St.
New York, NY 10016

What's Wrong with This Picture
National School Safety Center
4165 Thousand Oaks Blvd. Suite 290
Westlake Village, CA 91362

Secret Sounds Screaming: The Sexual Abuse of Children
Women Make Movies
462 Broadway Suite 500
New York, NY 10013

Touch
Illusion Theatre
528 Hennepin Ave. Suite 704
Minneapolis, MN 55403

BROCHURES/PAMPHLETS

Available from Missing and Exploited Children Clearinghouse
Division of Criminal Justice Services
Executive Park Tower
Albany, NY 12203

Child Protection (also in Spanish)
Child Protection Priorities in State Legislation
Just in Case . . . Your Child Is a Runaway (also in Spanish)
*Just in Case . . . Your Child Is a Victim of Sexual Abuse
or Exploitation*
My 8 Rules for Safety
How to Protect Your Child from Abduction by Strangers
Child Sexual Abuse Prevention
What to Do If Your Child Is Missing

Available from National Crime Prevention Council
1700 K St., NW, Second Floor
Washington, DC 20006

Raising Streetwise Kids
*The Art of Street Smarts: Knowing How to Protect
Yourself and Your Friends Makes Good Sense*

Available from Community Advocates for Safety and
Self-Reliance
4183 S.E. Division
Portland, OR 97202

Touch That Hurts: Talking with Children about Sexual Abuse

Available from Playing It Safe
123 Eileen Way
Syosset, NY 11791

Program Manuals
Safety Tips Brochure
Playing It Safe Certificate

Safety Stickers
Safety Phone Cards
Posters
Puppet Pals
Safety Songs

SAMPLE POPULAR BOOKS FOR CHILDREN

I Like You to Make Jokes with Me, But I Don't Want You to Touch Me
Ellen Bass
Carolina Wren Press
300 Barclay Rd.
Chapel Hill, NC 27514

It's MY Body
Lory Freeman
Parenting Press
Suite 600 7750 31st Ave. NE
Seattle, WA 98115

The Trouble with Secrets
Karen Johnson
Parenting Press
Suite 600 7750 31st Ave. NE
Seattle, WA 98115

SAMPLE OUTLINE OF A LECTURE ON MISSING CHILDREN FOR COLLEGE STUDENTS

Child Abductions and Missing Children: Myths and Realities
   An abductor is a psychotic human being, easily identifiable by children and adults.
   There are no long-term aftereffects of abductions for those who are found.
   It is only young, helpless children who are the prey of abductors.

Runaway children and adolescents are not targeted for abductions.

Parental abduction is not a serious matter and is not a form of child abuse.

Abductions don't happen here to the people I know—they happen somewhere else.

Violence in the Home and Community
Legal definition of incest
Incidence
Myths about incest
Psychological aspects of incest
Types of incest
Long-term adjustment of incest victims
Impact of incest on the family system
Counseling incest victims

Abuse of Power in Child Abductions

Issues in Victimization
Labelling
Blaming the victim
The "second" assault
Lack of support systems
"Just-world" hypothesis

Educational approaches for dealing with violence and victimization

Concluding comments

SAMPLE TERM-PAPER TOPICS FOR COLLEGE STUDENTS

- Children as witnesses in court cases on abductions
- Role of religion in counseling victims of abductions and sexual violence
- Treatment of post-traumatic stress disorder in child sexual abuse cases
- Media portrayal of sexual violence against children
- Developing a training module for high school teachers on child abductions and missing children

- Effects of childhood sexual abuse on children's behavior problems
- The "just-world" hypothesis explanation for why abductions occur
- Expert witness testimony in child abduction cases
- Methods for parents to teach preschoolers about abductions
- Community mental health centers and their role in assisting families of abducted children

Appendix D
Missing Children and Child Abductions: Resources for Therapeutic Intervention

TYPES OF PROFESSIONAL COUNSELORS

Prior to working with any professional counselor, individuals should know her or his training, experience, and licensing status. If the professional is licensed, clients should contact the state licensing board to confirm this information. If the professional is not licensed, clients may seek additional information from local universities, rape-crisis centers, and other organizations.

Psychologists

These counselors have received graduate training in diagnosing and treating a range of emotional problems and mental disorders. They may be specialists in clinical psychology, counseling psychology, and school psychology.

Psychiatrists

These professional counselors are physicians with a specialization in emotional disorders. They are the only professional counselors who are permitted to prescribe medications (e.g., antidepressants).

Psychiatric Social Workers

These counselors have earned at least a master's degree in a program that emphasizes mental health and counseling. They

also have special knowledge of legal and institutional requirements regarding abuse and resolution.

Psychiatric Nurses

These professional counselors have received training in a school
of nursing and have also received considerable medical training.

Pastoral Counselors

These counselors include priests, ministers, rabbis, nuns, and
other religious agents who have training in counsleing or therapeutic intervention.

Appendix E
What to Do if Your Child Is Missing

WHAT TO DO IF YOUR CHILD IS MISSING

Preparation

If a child be missing, the following data collected by parents will help law-enforcement personnel search for and identify the child when she or he is discovered:

1. Keep a complete description of the child. Include height, weight, hair color, eye color, any distinguishing features, date of birth, hearing or sight impairment, etc.

2. Take color photographs of your child at least every six months. Head and shoulder photos of high quality and from different angles.

3. Have dental charts prepared by your child's dentist. Accurate, up-to-date records, including x-rays.

4. Have medical records available or know how to access them. Know scars, birthmarks, broken bones.

5. Fingerprint your child. This can be arranged with your local police department. The police will give you a fingerprint card and maintain a record of the child's prints themselves.

145

Action

It is critical to act immediately should you suspect your child is missing. Check your house thoroughly, call your neighbors and friends to determine your child's whereabouts. If you cannot find your child, call the police immediately!

What to Tell the Police

1. Identify yourself and your location.

2. State: "Please send an officer. I want to report a missing child."

3. Provide the following information:

   a. child's name,

   b. date of birth,

   c. weight,

   d. unique identifiers (e.g., eyeglasses, pierced ears, braces),

   e. time child last seen, and

   f. clothing child was wearing.

4. Request that your child be entered immediately into the National Crime Information Center Missing Persons File. This procedure will help any law-enforcement agency in the United States identify and locate your child.

Appendix F
Sample Child Identification Sheet

The following information should be completed and updated as necessary by parents.

The sheet should be kept in a place that is easily accessible.

Name of Child:

Date of Birth:

Address:

School: Grade:

Complexion:

Hair Color and Type: Eye Color:

Glasses: Weight: Height: Build:

Speech: Marks, Scars:

Teeth: Name of Dentist:

Jewelry Worn:

Clothing sizes:

Overcoat:	Jacket:	Trousers:
Sweater:	Shoes:	Hat:
Dress:	Skirt:	Blouse:
Shirt:	Socks:	

Laundry Marks:

Labels in Clothing:

Health Problems:

Medication:

Name of Physicians:

Mother's Name:

Address:

Phone:

Father's Name:

Address:

Phone:

Appendix G
Recommendations for Further Reading

JOURNAL ARTICLES

Cole, W., and J. Bradford. (1992). "Abduction during Custody and Access Disputes." *Canadian Journal of Psychiatry* 37, 264–66.

Eccles, J., C. Midgley, A. Wigfield, C. Buchanan, D. Reuman, C. Flanagan, and D. Mac Iver. (1993). "Development during Adolescence." *American Psychologist* 48, 90–101.

Finkelhor, D., and J. Dziuba-Leatherman. (1994). "Victimization of Children." *American Psychologist* 49, 173–83.

Grief, G., and R. Heger, (1992). "Impact on Children of Abduction by a Parent: A Review of the Literature." *American Journal of Orthopsychiatry* 62, 599–604.

Heger, R., and G. Grief. (1991). "Abduction of Children by Their Parents: A Survey of the Problem." *Social Work* 36, 421–26.

———. (1993). "How Parentally Abducted Children Fare: An Interim Report on Families Who Recover Their Children." *Journal of Psychiatry and Law* 21, 373–83.

———. (1994). "Parental Abduction of Children from Interractial and Cross-Cultural Marriages." *Journal of Comparative Family Studies* 25, 135–42.

Hunt, P.,and M. Baird. (1990). "Children of Sex Rings." *Child Welfare* 69, 195–207.

Kendall-Tackett, K., L. Williams, and D. Finkelhor. (1993). "Impact of Sexual Abuse on Children: A Review and Synthesis of Recent Empirical Studies." *Psychological Bulletin* 11, 164–80.

Lang, R., and R. Frenzel. (1988). "How Sex Offenders Lure Children." *Annals of Sex Research* 1, 303–17.

Lanning, K. (1994). "Child Molesters: A Behavioral Analysis." *School Safety* (Spring): 12–17.

McGuire, J. (1994). "Re-Painting the Golden Gate Bridge: Coordination of Services for Abducted Children Reunited with Their Families." *Child and Adolescent Social Work Journal* 11, 149–64.

Palenski, J., and H. Launer. (1987). "The 'Process' of Running Away: A Redefinition." *Adolescence* 22, 347–62.

Peach, M., and D. Klass. (1987). "Special Issues in the Grief of Parents of Murdered Children." *Death Studies* 11, 81–88.

Poche, C. (1988). "Teaching Self-Protection to Children Using Television Techniques." *Journal of Applied Behavioral Analysis* 21, 253–61.

Scott, K. (1992). "Childhood Sexual Abuse: Impact on a Community's Mental Health Status." *Child Abuse and Neglect* 16, 285–95.

BOOKS AND BOOK CHAPTERS

Abrahms, S. (1983). *Children in the Crossfire: The Tragedy of Parental Kidnapping.* New York: Atheneum.

Bryant, C. (1992). "The Victimology of Children: A Transpersonal Conceptual Treatment Model." In E. Viano (ed)., *Critical Issues in Victimology: International Perpectives.* New York: Springer.

Conte, J., and L. Berliner. (1988). "The Impact of Child Sexual Abuse: Empirical Findings." In L. E. A. Walker (ed.), *Handbook on Sexual Abuse of Children.* New York: Springer.

Courtois, C. (1988). *Healing the Incest Wound: Adult Survivors in Therapy.* New York: Norton.

Eth, S., and R. Pynoos. (1985). *Post-Traumatic Stress Disorder in Children*. Washington: American Psychiatric Press.

Finkelhor, D., and A. Browne. (1988). "The Traumatogenic Effects of Child Sexual Abuse." In L. E. A.Walker (ed.), *Handbook on Sexual Abuse of Children*. New York: Springer.

Huttinger, B. (1984). *My Child Is Not Missing: A Parent's Guidebook for the Prevention and Recovery of Missing Children*. Plantation, FL: Child Safe Products.

Hyde, M., and L. Hyde. (1985). *Missing Children*. New York: Franklin Watts.

Leach, P. (1994). *Children First: What Our Society Must Do and Is Not Doing for Our Children Today*. New York: Knopf.

Newman, S. (1985). *Never Say Yes to a Stranger*. New York: Putnam.

Strickland, M. (1983). *How to Deal with a Parental Kidnapping*. Moorehaven, FL: Rainbow.

Terr, L. (1990). *Too Scared to Cry*. New York: Harper/Collins.

Appendix H
Recommendations for Parents for Reducing the Risk of Physical and Sexual Abuse of Children in Day-Care Centers

The following recommendations are not an absolute guarantee against day care center abuse. However, they will help to reduce the risk.

1. Involve yourself in the activities of the day-care center: volunteer to assist on field trips or in the center for several days or weeks.

2. Ensure that the day-care center provides opportunities for parents to visit regularly with no requirements to call first. Be sure that all areas of the day-care center welcome parents—that there are no areas off limits to parents.

3. Be sure that children are properly supervised during nap time. Staff must be in the room with the children.

4. Determine how the day-care center staff disciplines children. Which staff member is assigned to disciplining children? What discipline is used? Why is it used?

5. Learn the names of all day-care center staff. In addition, get to know nonstaff employees who come in contact with the children on a daily basis, such as bus drivers, janitors, and relatives of the day-care center providers. Be sure your child has limited contact with individuals who are not day-care center staff.

6. Demand to know the education and experience with children each staff member has. Be sure each staff member was screened for any criminal history in sexual or physical assault against children. Also inquire as to whether the staff members have been screened for substance abuse. You must inquire about all members of the day care center—including teacher's aides and volunteers.

7. Inquire about supervision of children using the bathroom facilities. Be certain that the bathrooms are not isolated from the rest of the day-care center. Inquire about which staff member takes children to the bathroom, for what purposes, and at what times during the day.

8. Inquire that the day-care center is fully licensed. Call your local department of social services and day-care licensing offices.

9. Ask for the day-care center's references; check these references carefully.

10. Contact the local police department and department of social services to determine whether any reports have been filed against the day-care center staff.

11. Listen carefully to your children about their experiences at the day-care center. Be sure to establish an atmosphere of trust in your home so your child can talk with you about all issues—including sensitive and embarrassing situations.

12. Be alert to any changes in your children's behavior: are they reluctant to go to the day-care center? Do they want to avoid a certain staff member at the day-care center? Are they asking unusual questions about sexuality? Are they acting out inappropriate sexal activity?

13. For preverbal as well as verbal children, be sure to examine them regularly. This should be done by you as well as by your child's pediatrician.

14. Be sure to explain to your children that he/she has the right to say *no* to any person who asks them to do something they do not want to do.

15. Teach your child that she/he should never have anyone at the day-care center touch them in the private parts of their body.

16. Teach your children to say *no* to anyone at the day-care center who wants to take their picture in a way that makes them feel uncomfortable. Be sure to tell your children that they should tell you if someone tries to take their picture.

17. Tell your child to say *no* to any person at the day care center who wants to drive them home or any other place. Your child must be taught to go *only* with you or your designate.

18. You and your child should select a "codeword" or "codephrase" with which the child is familiar (e.g., a favorite food, TV show). Tell your child that if he or she is approached by someone who uses the codeword, such as in a medical emergency, that this means it is safe to accompany this individual. Change the codeword after each use to prevent it from being inadvertently disclosed to other individuals. Teach your child never to tell anyone the codeword.

19. Follow the advice offered in chapter 5 concerning parental responsibility in teaching children about safety.

20. Be alert to the following physical signs in your child: changes in bed-wetting, nightmares, or other sleep disturbances; bruises, rashes, unexplained or poorly explained injuries; bleeding, itching, or pain in the genital area; and modifications in toilet-training habits.

21. If you suspect physical or sexual abuse of your child: stop taking your child to the center; immediately seek out medical attention for your child; immediately notify the police and any other law-enforcement agency;

notify the child-protection services and other social-service agencies; have other parents alerted to the issue; discuss the need for therapeutic intervention for your child and your family; and keep your child's and your identity confidential should media attention be given to this issue.

About the Authors

Honorable James N. Tedisco

James N. Tedisco has been a member of the New York State Assembly since 1982. In his first year in the assembly, Mr. Tedisco was appointed Ranking Republican member on the Committee on Children and Families. He also served on the assembly committee on Aging and Education. In 1983, as a result of his work on behalf of missing children, Assemblymember Tedisco was appointed Chairperson of the Assembly Republican Task Force on Missing Children. Under Mr. Tedisco's leadership and guidance, the Task Force (1) conducted statewide public hearings to address the need for legislative and community action; (2) worked with state's media and other groups to develop public information and prevention programs; (3) publicized services for families of missing children; (4) examined the effectiveness of existing programs that deal with missing children; (5) introduced state legislation to supplement the federal Missing Children Act, and (6) coordinated efforts of local, state, and federal law enforcement agencies in missing children cases. Mr. Tedisco has also been a member of the Assembly Committee on Mental Health.

Mr. Tedisco worked in the field of education from 1973 to 1982, first as a guidance counselor and then as a special education teacher. He earned his B.S. degree in psychology from Union College, Schenectady, New York and his M.A. degree in special education from the College of St. Rose, Albany, New York.

Dr. Michele Paludi

Michele A. Paludi, Ph.D., is a developmental psychologist specializing in the psychology of women and victimization. A considerable amount of her research has focused on academic and workplace sexual harassment, especially the psychological impact of these forms of sexual victimization on individuals.

Dr. Paludi is Principal of Michele Paludi & Associates, Consultants in Sexual Harassment, and offers education and training in issues related to sexual harassment at elementary and secondary schools, colleges, and organizations. In addition, she is an expert witness for academic and court proceedings involving sexual harassment. She was a member of Governor Mario Cuomo's Task Force on Sexual Harassment.

Dr. Paludi has held faculty positions at Franklin and Marshall College, Kent State University, Hunter College, and Union College, where she has taught courses in child and adolescent development, gender, and violence and victimization.

She has collaborated with Assemblymember Tedisco as his Legislator Advisor on Women's Issues.

Index